RETAIN

SPORTS AND PASTIMES

OF

SCOTLAND

SPORTS AND PASTIMES

OF

SCOTLAND

HISTORICALLY ILLUSTRATED

BY

ROBERT SCOTT FITTIS

"The heart-cheering pleasure of the fields,
The choice delight of heroes and of kings."
Somerville's "Field Sports."

"By sports like these are all their cares beguiled."
Goldsmith's "Traveller."

EP PUBLISHING LIMITED
1975

Republished 1975 by EP Publishing Limited
East Ardsley, Wakefield
West Yorkshire, England

First published 1891 by Alexander Gardner

Copyright © 1975 EP Publishing Limited

ISBN 0 7158 1106 1

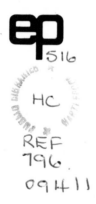

Please address all enquiries to
EP Publishing Limited (address as above)

Printed in Great Britain by
REDWOOD BURN LIMITED
Trowbridge & Esher

PREFACE.

___

IT is hoped that no reader will expect to find in this book anything more than what the title-page professes it to embody. The compilation is entirely outside the category of practical Manuals and Handbooks of Sports, many of which exist and are deservedly popular. Its sole object is to set forth a sort of history, somewhat after (though confessedly a long way behind) the model of Strutt's *Sports and Pastimes of the People of England*: "only this and nothing more."

The compilation has been the pleasing labour of years. Portions have previously appeared in print here and there; but these have been much amplified with new matter; and, so far as I am aware, the book, as it now stands, is the only one dealing with the generality of Scottish Sports on the same lines. I trust it will be found both interesting and useful, as illustrative of varied phases of the habits, manners, and customs of byegone generations of Scotsmen of all ranks and classes.

R. S. F.

CONTENTS.

SPORTS AND PASTIMES.

CHAPTER I.

THE OLD SCOTTISH WILD CATTLE.

Mightiest of all the beasts of chase,
　　That roam in woody Caledon,
Crashing the forest in his race,
　　The Mountain Bull comes thundering on !

Fierce, on the hunters' quiver'd band,
　　He rolls his eyes of swarthy glow,
Spurns, with black hoof and horn, the sand,
　　And tosses high his mane of snow.
　　　　　　　　Scott's " Cadyow Castle."

N the remote and misty past,—in epochs far beyond the ken of history, those pre-historic times
which stretch back indefinitely to the emergence
of our island from the bosom of the sea,—various species
of wild and savage animals were common in Britain,
partly contemporaneously, and partly in succession to
each other, according to the climatic changes, most of
which races have been long extinct in this country.　The
fact of their existence is attested by their remains found
chiefly in the limestone caverns and the river deposits.
The elephant and the rhinoceros grazed on British soil,
and the hippopotamus wandered on the banks of British

rivers. The moose-deer or elk once roamed here, though in small numbers. The rein-deer are believed to have spread over Britain and Ireland, towards the close of what is known as the glacial period. Ancient tradition asserts that in some distant age the Norwegians were wont to cross over to Scotland for the purpose of hunting the rein-deer! And tradition is so far supported in this story by an olden authority of fair repute, the *Orkneyinga Saga*, which states explicitly that the Norse lords of the Orkneys were accustomed to pass over to Caithness to enjoy the chase of the rein-deer. "The Jarls of Orkney were in the habit of crossing over to Caithness almost every summer, and there hunting in the wilds the red deer and the rein-deer:" and those Jarls [Earls] are said to have been Ronald and Harold, who lived in the middle of the twelfth century,—though we suspect the date of the existence of rein-deer in Caithness is rather too recent. Numerous remains of the rein-deer have been discovered there and in other parts of the country. In Perthshire, during drainage operations at the Loch of Marlee, many years ago, the horns and some of the leg-bones of a rein-deer were found. It should also be remembered that the rein-deer moss is still common in Scotland. The re-introduction of the rein-deer has been attempted in modern times, both on the hills of Athole, Perthshire, and in Mar Forest, Aberdeenshire; but in each case the project failed,—the animals having died soon after being liberated in the wilds.

It is believed that the elk and the rein-deer, or other animals of the deer tribe, were contemporaneous in Britain with carnivorous enemies—two species of lions, one greater and the other smaller in structure; a species of the leopard or panther; the hyæna; the grisly and brown bears, etc. Most of the larger beasts of prey were ultimately exterminated, perhaps by a constantly-increasing diminution of food, following the total separation of our island from the Continent of Europe. The lions, the leopard, the hyæna disappeared ; but the brown bear survived until long after the Roman invasion. In the *Sylvæ Caledonia*,—the great Caledonian Forest which overshadowed a vast extent of Scotland beyond the Forth, covering the vales of Menteith and Strathearn, and away across Athole and Lochaber, and which proved so formidable an obstacle to the progress of the Roman arms northward,—the blue-painted Pict could vary his fierce contest against the " masters of the world " with scarce lesser war against bears, wolves, boars, and those wild white cattle whose chase was the most exciting and perilous of all. The existence of the brown bear in Britain during the Roman times is established beyond the possibility of doubt. The animal was hunted by the Romans of the occupation : it was captured alive, and sent over the sea to Rome for the savage purposes of the amphitheatre. The Romans, writes Plutarch, "transported bears from Britain to Rome, where they had them in great admiration." The bears were used otherwise than for the ordinary sport of the populace of the Eternal City. It was the practice to crucify " malefactors "—probably in many cases Christian martyrs—in the circus, and then to let loose British bears to lacerate and devour the living victims nailed to the cross ! The poet Martial, in his 7th epigram, mentions the barbarous custom,—how that Laureolus, a noted robber, was crucified on the stage, in a drama, and torn to pieces by " a *Caledonian bear.*" Such was one of the many refinements of cruelty by which the vaunted Roman civilization was disgraced ! Centuries after the Roman occupation of Britain had ceased, the brown bear was still found in the island. An old Welsh manuscript states that the bear was authoritatively reckoned among the beasts of chase, and its flesh was considered as equal to that of the hare and the boar. To this day different localities in the Principality are called by names referring to the bear. In regard to England generally,—about the year 750, Archbishop Egbert wrote in his *Penitentiale* that "when any one strikes a wild beast with an arrow, and it escapes and is found dead three days afterwards, if a hound, a wolf, a fox, or a *bear*, or any other wild beast hath begun to feed upon it, let no Christian touch it." In the reign of Edward the Confessor, the town of Norwich was bound to furnish to the King one bear annually, and six dogs for the baiting of it : so it is entered in Doomsday Book : although doubt may be expressed whether the native bear was not extirpated in England prior to the era of the Norman Conquest. The bear-baiting which continued so long a popular pastime in England was at first supplied from the native race ; but afterwards bears for that sport were imported from the Continent.

Martial, as we have seen, speaks of the Caledonian bear. In Scotland the brown bear seems to have lingered longer than in the southern portion of the island. The rugged nature of the country, especially of the Highlands, afforded every facility for the shelter of wild beasts. Historical writers of the sixteenth century specify bears as having existed numerously in Scotland in ancient times, though the period of their extirpation is not indicated. Thus, Bishop Lesley says that the Caledonian Forest was once full of bears : and Camden, in his *Britannia*, writes that Athole was "a country fruitful enough, having woody vallies where once the Caledonian Forest (dreadful for its dark intricate windings, and for its dens of bears, and its huge, wild, thick-maned bulls)," had extended itself far and near in these parts. Traditions of the bear are still remembered in the north, where it is distinguished as the *Magh-Ghamhainn*—"the paw calf," and also under the more general term of *beiste*, or "the monster"—as—*Ruigh-na-beiste*, "The Monster's Slope," and *Loch-na-beiste* "The Monster's Lake." The surname of the Clan Forbes is said to have arisen in connection with the chase of the bear. An Irish chieftain, Ochonchar, came to Scotland, and hearing that a district in Aberdeenshire was ravaged by a bear, he went thither, tracked the destroyer to its lair, and was successful in putting it to death, for which exploit he was rewarded with lands, and the title of *Forbear* or *Forbeiste* was given him, while he was also granted three bears' heads as an armorial cognizance, which has ever since been borne by his descendants. Another version of the legend is to the effect that the hero killed the bear to obtain the hand of a beautiful heiress, named Bess or Elizabeth, and on accomplishing his object he assumed the name of "For Bess." A third version relates that a boar, not a bear, having devoured nine young women at a spring in the parish of Auchindoir, Aberdeenshire, it was "slain by a young man of the name of Forbes, the lover of one of the young women, and a stone with a boar's head cut on it, was set up to preserve the remembrance of his gallantry and courage. The stone," continues the Old Statistical writer, "was removed by Lord Forbes to his house of Putachie ; and it is from this circumstance that a boar's head is quartered in the arms of the family ;"—a mistake, the Forbes arms being three bears' heads. The spring where the tragedy happened was thenceforth known as the "Nine Maidens' Well." Ochonchar's slaughter of the bear is assigned to the eleventh century—the year 1057 ; but the brown bear must have become extinct in Scotland considerably earlier than that date. The main legend is a fair example of the turn for finding out a punning or familiar explanation of the names of persons and places, which was common in unlettered times. An instance of the same thing occurs in the derivation of " Buccleugh " :—

> ———Old Buccleugh the name did gain
> When in the cleuch the buck was ta'en.

King Kenneth Macalpin, as we are told, was hunting in Ettrick Forest, when the buck standing at bay in a hollow into which the monarch and his attendants, being on horseback, could not descend, a native of the country, a banished man, who followed the chase on foot, clambered down, and ran in upon the deer. Possessing great strength and daring, he seized it by the horns, and, throwing it upon his back, ascended the steep hill-side with his struggling burden, and flung it down before the King, who thereupon named him *Buccleugh*. Still another example will be given at a subsequent stage.

The ancient Celtic tribes of Scotland were much devoted to the chase, from which they derived a large portion of their subsistence: the wild hog, with which the country abounded, being one of their chief beasts of pursuit, notwithstanding that the sow appears to have been somehow associated with their mythology, and its figure is found on most of the sculptured stones,—hence the conjecture has been hazarded that originally it was worshipped here as in Egypt of old.* In the Perthshire vale of Glenshee there was once a famous boar-hunt, which, because it

---

* An image of the Caledonian boar stood in the Hippodrome of Constantinople ; and when the blind Emperor Isaac Angelus Comnenus was restored to his throne, in 1203, he caused the statue to be removed to his Palace, in the belief that its presence near his person would avert sedition.

proved fatal to the best-beloved of the Fingalian heroes, has been commemorated in song by one of Albin's olden bards. Diarmad, the son of Duine, was the nephew of Fingal, by the mother's side, and was the handsomest warrior in the train of the King of Morven, whose jealousy and hatred, however, he had the misfortune to kindle. Brave, noble Diarmad (so sung the bard) was full of strength and valour ; his might in battle was as a wintry torrent rushing on resistlessly : fair his cheek, red his lip, blue and grey blended in his clear eye, and long locks of yellow waved over his shoulders. Fingal's hate was moved against him ; but it was dissembled, and never found vent until a great hunt was held in Glenshee, where the sounds of deer and elk were ever heard, and where the stream winds at the foot of Ben Gulbin, among the grassy knolls and grey mossy cairns, on which the sunshine sweetly beams. Thither came the Fingalians,—Diarmad accompanying the "king of men." They climbed the hill with their dogs, and the great boar of Ben Gulbin was roused from his darksome cave. Fierce was the aged wild boar that issued in his wrath from the lofty echoing rocks. He sought safety in flight, but being hemmed in by the hunters and their eager pack, he turned furiously upon them, scattering the hounds and defying sword and spear. Diarmad, ever fearless and intrepid, sprung forward to the encounter. His spear shivered in splinters on the beast's thick hide, but drawing his thin-leaved sword, of all the arms most crowned with victory, he killed the monster with repeated strokes rapid as the levin-bolt. Sad was Fingal at the sight. It grieved his soul that Diarmad had not fallen a victim,—that the youth should even have emerged unwounded from the struggle. Long sat the King on the hill-side, musing in gloomy silence ; and, then pointing to the enormous carcase stretched on the grass,

he said—"Diarmad, measure the boar from snout to heel,
that we may know its length." Diarmad did so. He
measured the boar by treading with his bare feet along its
back. "Measure it again, from heel to snout, against the
bristles," cried the King. This was also done. But the
poisonous bristles pierced Diarmad's naked soles, and the
venom working quickly into his blood, he fell beside the
boar, and died: and so Fingal was revenged. "Valorous
chief!" laments the bard, "lightly may the clod rest upon
thy golden locks! I stand by thy grave, like a leafless,
sapless bough amid the whistling blast of sorrow that
scatters the withered twigs around Diarmad's bed at the
bottom of Ben Gulbin. Though green was the hill when
first we approached it, yet red it is this night with the
blood of the youthful champion." This is the legend of
the hunting of Glenshee: and somewhat may be traced in
it of analogy with classic fable; for Achilles was vulnerable
only in the heel, and Adonis, the beloved of the Cyprian
goddess, was slain by a boar. The clan Campbell claim
their descent from Diarmad: they are called in Gaelic
song *Sliochd Diarmad an Tuirc*—"the race of Diarmad
who slew the boar:" and their heraldic crest is the boar's
head. A curious entry in the Sheriff of Forfar's Accounts
for the year 1263 would seem to indicate that by the time
of Alexander III. the wild boar had become scarce in the
country. The Sheriff notes that he expended $4\frac{1}{2}$ chalders
of corn for the wild boars, *porci silvestres:* upon which
Professor Innes asks:—"Are we to conclude from this last
that the native wild boar of the Caledonian Forest had
become extinct or scarce in the valley of Strathmore, and
that a supply was reared for sport?"* The wild hog
seems to have long haunted the far Highland wastes,

---

* *Scotland in the Middle Ages*, p. 123.

though its numbers were fast diminishing. In Scott's *Highland Widow*, Elspat of the Tree, recounting to her son reminiscences of her native Kintail, tells him that "the white-tusked boar, the chase of which the brave loved best, was yet to be roused in those western solitudes." Eventually the wild hog shared the fate of the brown bear.

The ravages of the Wolf provoked Scottish Parliaments of the fifteenth century to pass decrees for its extirpation. But even the wolf was outlived by remnants of the white cattle which, from time immemorial had haunted the Scottish woods ; and, indeed, to this day, survivors of this race are preserved in several parts of our island. The indigenous wild ox of Britain was the *Urus ;* but whether the later breed of wild cattle, and, in particular, the Scottish Bison or White Bull, can be held as sprung of the aboriginal stock, we do not pretend to judge. It has been supposed that the Urus became extinct in England within the pre-historic period, but that it still subsisted in the regions north of the Tweed. At all events, the wild White Bull appears to have been in Scotland from very early days, and was contemporaneous with various beasts of prey, to which it must have proved a sturdy and dreaded opponent. Without troubling ourselves with vexed questions of breed and descent, let us say that there is abundant and indisputable evidence to show that, for many ages, herds of wild cattle were numerous on both sides of the Border. The "Celtic shorthorn" is understood to have been the domesticated British ox during the Roman occupation ; but wild cattle in England are spoken of in records dating more than eight centuries ago. The "Forest Laws" of King Canute, who reigned from 1014 to 1036, state that "there are also a great number of cattle which, although they live within the limits of the forest, and are subject to the charge and care of the middle sort of men, or Regardors, nevertheless cannot at all be reputed beasts of the forest as wild horses, *bubali* [buffaloes, or wild bulls], wild cows," and so forth.   An earlier reference occurs in Wales.   The "*Leges Wallicæ*," or Welsh Laws of King Howell the Good, enacted about 942-3, mention white cattle with red ears, which were to be given in compensation for certain offences committed against the Welsh Princes.   Matthew Paris, in his *Lives of the Abbots of St. Albans*, relates how, in the days of Edward the Confessor, "there abounded throughout the whole of Ciltria [the Chiltrens] spacious woods, thick and large, the habitation of numerous and various beasts, wolves, boars, forest bulls [*tauri sylvestres*], and stags."   The historian Fitz-Stephen, says, about 1174, that "close at hand" to London, " lies an immense forest, woody ranges, hiding places of wild beasts, of stags, of fallow deer, of boars, and of [*tauri sylvestres*] forest bulls."   Subsequent records speak of wild cattle in other parts of England; and tradition goes as far back as the oldest writing extant. The ballad of " Sir Guy of Warwick," dating at least in the sixteenth century, tells how the hero slew a great wild cow (called "the Dun-cow of Dunsmore heath") in the time of King Athelstan, who reigned from 925 to 940: and although the ballad as such cannot be regarded as competent authority, yet it doubtless preserves a very ancient popular belief which coincides in the main with well-authenticated facts.

We now pass to Scotland, where the wild white cattle have been well known.   One or two references to the race appear in Ossian's Poems ; as, for example, in " Fingal " (Macpherson's version):—" Long had they strove for the spotted [the original has *spotless*] bull that lowed on Golbun's echoing heath.   Each claimed him as

his own. Death was often at the point of their steel.
Side by side the heroes fought; the strangers of ocean
fled. Whose name was fairer on the hill than the name
of Cairbar and Grudar? But, ah! why ever lowed the
bull on Golbun's echoing heath? They saw him leaping
like *snow*." And, again—"I went and divided the herd.
One snow-white bull remained. I gave that bull to
Cairbar." But the most ample and distinct account of
the wild white cattle is given by Hector Boece, in his
Scotorum Historiæ, which was first published in 1526;
and his account has been repeated by succeeding writers.
" In this wood"—the great Caledonian Forest, says he,
" were some time white bulls, with crisp and curling manes,
like fierce lions; and though they seemed meek and
tame in the remanent figure of their bodies, yet were
more wild than any other beasts; and had such hatred
against the society and company of men, that they came
never in the woods or lesuris [pastures] where they found
any feet or hand thereof; and many days after they eat
not of the herbs that were touched or handled by men.
Thir bulls were so wild that they were never taken but
[without] sleight and crafty labour, and so impatient, that
after their taking they died for importable [insupportable]
dolour. As soon as any man invaded thir bulls, they
rushed with so terrible press on him that they dang him
to the earth, taking no fear of hounds, sharp lances, nor
other most penetrative weapons." Boece then tells a
story of the narrow escape of King Robert Bruce, while,
with a small train, he was hunting the wild bull in the
Forest, and how the King's deliverer received the name
of *Turnbull* for his prowess at the critical moment. "For
after the beast felt himself sore wounded by the hunters,
he rushed upon the King, who having no weapon left in
his hand wherewith to defend himself, he had surely

perished, if rescue had not come. Howbeit in this distress one came running unto him, who overthrew the bull by plain force, and held him down till the hunters came that killed him outright. For this valiant act the King endowed the aforesaid party with great possessions, and his lineage is to this day called of the Turnbulls, because he overturned the beast, and saved the King's life, by such great prowess and manhood." Of course, the story, so far as relates to the origin of the surname, bears the same mint-mark as that of Forbes or Buccleugh ; although the incident of, the King's rescue has nothing improbable in it. This Turnbull, it is farther said, fell in a singular manner at Halidon Hill, in July, 1333. Immediately before the battle joined, he, accompanied by a large and ferocious mastiff, advanced towards the English army, and challenged any soldier to single combat. A Norfolk knight, Sir Richard Benhale, encountered the bold Scot, and being first assailed by the dog, killed it at a blow, and then engaging Turnbull, hewed off both his left hand and his head. With regard to the wild bulls, Bishop Lesley, in his *History*, published in 1578, gives a description of the animals similar to that of Boece, and adds that in his day such cattle were preserved in the parks of Stirling, Cumbernauld, and Kincardine.

At the baptism of James VI., in the Chapel of Stirling Castle, the Earl of Bedford attended, as representative of Queen Elizabeth : and on the following day the English party were entertained with " the hunting of the wild bull," in Stirling park, at which Queen Mary was present. In 1570, certain retainers of the Regent Lennox were charged with " having slain and destroyed the deer in John Fleming's forest of Cumbernauld and the white kye and bulls of the said forest, to the great destruction of police and hinder of the commonweal; for" adds the document quoted (*Calendar*, 1570, No 1418) "that kind of kye and bulls has been kept there many years in the said forest, and the like was not maintained in any other part of this isle of Albion, as is well known."

The chief haunts of the wild white cattle of Scotland had been the old forests, which, however, were gradually destroyed, partly by the ravages of war, and partly by the extension of cultivation consequent on the increase and spread of population, so that the herds were deprived of their accustomed and necessary shelter. The breed would seem to have been extirpated generally in the Highlands sooner than in the low country, leaving only to after-days a hazy traditional recollection in which superstition mingled its dreams and terrors,—the white bull merging into a mythical "water-bull," which, with malevolent powers akin to those of the "kelpie" or water-horse, was supposed to hover about small lochs amid heathy deserts and rocky solitudes and the remnants of ancient woods. "It is easy," say the brothers John Sobieski and Charles Edward Stuart (in their *Lays of the Deer Forest*, Vol II., p. 222) "to resolve this fable into the associations of the last animal of the district, exaggerated by its mysterious seclusion and ferocious nature. The wild bull, like the stag, is fond of deep solitude, water, and marshy places, and in summer retires to remote lakes and rivers, loving to stand in the water, and wallow in the mire. When the wild cattle were reduced to here and there a single individual, his haunt would be often—in some seasons always—about the margins of the small marshy lakes in the depths of the woods, where, formidable to the hunter, and a terror to women and children, he would soon become the minotaur of the neighbourhood, and hence the superstitions associated with all those little lakes in the Highlands called *Bull-Lochs*." In the Lowlands the few survivors of the race fared otherwise ; for at some places in the south of Scotland, the enclosures—parks and policies—which came to be formed around baronial castles and mansions, preserved what remained of the once numerous herds. Thus, a number of these cattle were confined in the park of Cadyow Castle, on the banks of the Avon, before its confluence with the Clyde. There the Hamiltons have ruled for centuries, but the castle went to ruin after the civil wars of Queen Mary's time. The Caledonian Forest had spread over this district, and scattered fragments of it still remain, in the shape of lofty, broad-topped oaks, darkening the course of the stream. The Cadyow domain was granted to the Hamilton family by King Robert Bruce, who used to hunt in its woods ; and probably it was there that Turnbull rescued him from the infuriated wild bull. Succeeding sovereigns occasionally enjoyed the same sport in the same locality, and it is known that James IV. did so about the year 1500. Unvarying tradition declares that a herd of the white cattle existed at Cadyow from the time of the Bruce's grant to the Hamiltons ; and there a herd remains to this day.

In 1764, Mr. John Wilson, an ingenious schoolmaster in the west of Scotland, published at Glasgow his loco-descriptive poem of *The Clyde*, in which there is a passage devoted to these cattle as they then existed :—

> Where these high walls round wide inclosures run,
> Forbid the winter, and invite the sun,
> Wild strays the race of bisons, white as snow,
> Hills, dales, and woods re-echo when they low.
> No houses lodge them, and no milk they yield,
> Save to their calves ; nor turn the furrowed field :
> At pleasure through the spacious pastures stray ;
> No keeper know, nor any guide obey ;

Nor round the dairy with swelled udders stand,
Or, lowing, court the milkmaid's rosy hand.
But, mightiest of his race, the bull is bred ;
High o'er the rest he rears his armed head,
The monarch of the drove, his sullen roar,
Shakes Clyde with all his rocks from shore to shore.
The murdered sounds in billowy surges come,
Deep, dismal as the death-denouncing drum,
When some dark traitor, 'mid an armed throng,
His bier the sable sledge, is dragged along.
Not prouder looked the Thunderer when he bore
The fair Europa from the Tyrian shore :
The beauteous females that his nod obey,
Match the famed heifers of the god of day.

The brothers Stuart described the animals in 1848, when they were about 60 in number. They were " of a pure white colour, their eyes dark blue, their noses black, the ears tipped and lined with the same colour, the horns white, tipped with black, and the feet generally speckled, according as the hair above the hoof is black or white. The bulls have now in a great measure lost their manes, and the cows are horned or 'humble' indifferently. The general size of the animal is a degree larger than the West Highland cattle, fat bulls of seven or eight years old weighing about 55 to 60 stones ; cows full-grown from 28 to 35 stones. Although by long limit to the semi-detached state of an inclosed park, familiarised to the sight of man, the animals have lost their original ferocity, the bulls are fierce when pursued, and at all times shy." * An account of the habits of these animals has also been given by the Rev. W. Patrick, in the *Quarterly Journal of Agriculture* :—

I am inclined to believe that the Hamilton breed of cattle is the oldest in Scotland, or perhaps in Britain. Although Lord Tankerville has said they

---

* *Lays of the Deer Forest*, Vol. II., p. 225.

have "no wild habits," I am convinced from personal observation, that this is one of their peculiar features. In browsing their extensive pasture, they always keep close together, never scattering or straggling over it,—a peculiarity which does not belong to the Kyloe, or any other breed, from the wildest or most inhospitable regions of the Highlands. The white cows are also remarkable for their systematic manner of feeding. At different periods of the year their tactics are different, but by those acquainted with their habits they are always found about the same part of the forest at the same hour of the day. In the height of summer, they always bivouac for the night towards the northern extremity of the forest ; from this point they start in the morning, and browse to the southern extremity, and return at sunset to their old rendezvous ; and during these perambulations they always feed *en masse.*

The bulls are seldom ill-natured, but when they are so, they display a disposition more than ordinarily savage, cunning, pertinacious, and revengeful. A poor bird-catcher, when exercising his vocation among the "Old Oaks," as the park is familiarly called, chanced to be attacked by a savage bull. By great exertion he gained a tree before his assailant made up to him. Here he had occasion to observe the habits of the animal. It did not roar or bellow, but merely grunted, the whole body quivered with passion and savage rage, and he frequently attacked the tree with his head and hoofs. Finding all to no purpose, he left off the vain attempt, began to browse, and removed to some distance from the tree. The bird-catcher, tried to descend, but his watchful Cerberus was again instantly at his post, and it was not until after six hours' imprisonment, and various bouts at "bo-peep" as above, that the unfortunate man was relieved by some shepherds with their dogs. A writer's apprentice, who had been at the village of Quarter on business, and who returned by the "Oaks" as a "near-hand cut," was also attacked by one of these savage brutes, near the northern extremity of the forest. He was fortunate, however, in getting up a tree, but was watched by the bull, and kept there, during the whole of the night, and till near two o'clock next day.

These animals are never taken and killed like other cattle, but are always shot in the field. I once went to see a bull and some cows destroyed in this manner,—not by any means for the sake of the sight, but to observe the manner and habits of the animal under peculiar circumstances. When the shooters approached, they, as usual, scampered off in a body, then stood still, tossed their heads on high, and seemed to snuff the wind ; the manœuvre was often repeated, till they got so hard pressed (and seemingly having a sort of half-idea of the tragedy which was to be performed), they at length ran furiously in a mass, always preferring the sides of the fence and sheltering situations, and dexterously taking advantage of any inequality in the ground, or other circumstances, to conceal themselves from the assailing foe. In their flight, the bulls, or stronger of the flock, always took the lead ; a smoke ascended from them which could be seen at a great distance ; and they were often so close together, like sheep, that a carpet would have covered them. The cows which had young, on the first "tug of war," all retreated to the thickets where their calves were concealed ; from prudential motives, they are never, if possible, molested. These and other wild habits I can testify to being inherent in the race, and are well known to all who have an opportunity of acquainting themselves with them.

The number of these cattle kept at Cadyow Castle, in October, 1874, was 45 ; of which 30 were in the park, and 15 bulls and steers were in an adjoining pasture field. In June, 1877, the numbers remained much the same.

At Drumlanrig Castle, in Dumfriesshire, one of the seats of the Queensberry family, a herd of wild white cattle was kept until about the year 1780, when, on account of their ferocity, they were sold to an English nobleman by the fourth and last Duke of Queensberry, and removed across the Border. Mr. Pennant, when at Drumlanrig, in 1772, saw these cattle, and has described them in his *Tour :*—

In my walks about the park, see the white breed of wild cattle, derived from the native race of the country ; and still retain the primeval savageness and ferocity of their ancestors ; were more shy than any deer ; ran away on the appearance of any of the human species, and even set off at full gallop on the least noise ; so that I was under the necessity of going very softly under the shelter of trees or bushes to get a near view of them ; during summer they keep apart from all other cattle, but in severe weather hunger will compel them to visit the outhouses in search of food. The keepers are obliged to shoot them, if any are wanted : if the beast is not killed on the spot, it runs at the person who gave the wound, and who is forced, in order to save himself, to fly for safety to the intervention of some tree.

These cattle are of a middle size, have very long legs, and the cows are fine horned : the orbits of the eyes and the tips of the noses are black ; but the bulls have lost the manes attributed to them by Boethius.

Upwards of half-a-century ago, a herd of wild white cattle, with black ears, muzzles, and hoofs, was kept in one of the Parks attached to Blair Castle, Perthshire, the seat of the Duke of Athole. How long they had been there we have not ascertained ; but in 1834 it was resolved to dispose of the herd, and accordingly it was sold,—part being purchased by the Marquis of Breadalbane, and part by the Duke of Buccleuch. But neither at Taymouth Castle nor Dalkeith Palace were the animals long preserved. A sort of half-breed from this herd is still kept at Kilmory House, Argyleshire, belonging to Sir John Powlett Orde.

At Ardrossan Castle, in Ayrshire, a herd of the white cattle was introduced, about 1750, by Alexander, tenth Earl of Eglinton. What their number was is uncertain ; but they were gradually diminished by shooting to about a dozen, when, in 1820 Hugh, the twelfth Earl, ordered them to be destroyed, which was accordingly done.

In another part of the same county,—at Auchencruive, a herd of the white cattle was introduced by Lord Cathcart about the same time as they were brought to Ardrossan, namely, in the middle of the last century. In 1763, however, Auchencruive estate was sold to Mr. Oswald, and he previous to his death, in 1784, caused the wild cattle to be killed on account of their dangerous propensities.

At Chillingham Castle, in Northumberland, the patrimony of the Earl of Tankerville, a park with wild cattle is distinctly mentioned in records of the year 1292, while the "great wood" of Chillingham is spoken of as early as 1220. The park of 1292 comprised 1500 acres ; and at present, excluding woods, it contains 1100 acres. There can be little doubt that from the end of the fifteenth century down to the present day, Chillingham has possessed a herd of the ancient white cattle of Britain "that has remained secluded in what still exists as a wild tract of country amongst the Cheviot hills on the bounds of Scotland, where they have scarcely been disturbed in their quiet possession until startled by the whistle of the railway engine." When Mr. Pennant visited the Castle in 1772, he noted that " in the park are between thirty and forty wild cattle, of the same kind with those described at Drumlanrig." After the publication of *Castle Dangerous*, Sir Walter Scott received an interesting letter on the subject of the Chillingham cattle, which he appended to the revised edition of the novel :—

When it is wished to kill any of the cattle at Chillingham, the keeper goes into the herd on horseback, in which way they are quite accessible, and, singling out his victim, takes aim with a large rifle-gun, and seldom fails in bringing him down. If the poor animal makes much bellowing in his agony, and especially if the ground be stained with his blood, his companions become very furious, and are themselves, I believe, accessory to his death. After which they fly off to a distant part of the park, and he is drawn away on a sledge. Lord Tankerville is very tenacious of these singular animals ; he will on no account part with a living one, and hardly allows of a sufficient number being killed, to leave pasturage for those that remain.

It happened on one occasion, three or four years ago, that a party visiting at the Castle, among whom were some *men of war*, who had hunted buffaloes in foreign parts, obtained permission to do the keeper's work, and shoot one of the wild cattle. They sallied out on horseback, and, duly equipped for the enterprise, attacked their object. The poor animal received several wounds, but none of them proving fatal, he retired before his pursuers, roaring with pain and rage, till, planting himself against a wall or tree, he stood at bay, offering a front of defiance. In this position the youthful heir of the Castle, Lord Ossulston, rode up to give him the fatal shot. Though warned of the danger of approaching near to the enraged animal, and especially of firing without first having turned his horse's head in a direction to be ready for flight, he discharged his piece ; but ere he could turn his horse round to make his retreat, the raging beast had plunged his immense horns into his flank. The horse staggered, and was near falling, but recovering by a violent effort he extricated himself from his infuriated pursuer, making off with all the speed his wasting strength supplied, his entrails meanwhile dragging on the ground, till at length he fell, and died at the same moment. The animal was now close upon his rear, and the young Lord would unquestionably have shared the fate of his unhappy steed, had not the keeper, deeming it full time to conclude the *day's diversion*, fired at the instant.

His shot brought the beast to the ground, and running in with his large knife, he put a period to his existence.

This scene of gentlemanly pastime was viewed from a turret of the Castle by Lady Tankerville and her female visitors. Such a situation for the mother of the young hero was anything but enviable.

Particulars are known of the Chillingham herd at different periods, commencing with the year 1692. In that year the herd numbered 28 animals. In 1772, Mr. Pennant reckoned 30 or 40. In 1838, the number was 80; in 1861, it was 50; in 1873, it was 64; in 1874, it was 71; in 1875, it was 62; and in July, 1877, the herd had decreased to 59. An authority quoted in Maxwell's *Border Tales* describes the cattle as "invariably white; muzzle black; the whole of the inside of the ear, and about one-third of the outside from the tip downwards, red; horns white, with black tips, very fine, and bent upwards: some of the bulls have a thin upright mane, about an inch and a-half or two inches long; the weight of the oxen is from 35 to 45 stone, and the cows from 25 to 35 stone." Formerly a portion of the cattle were black-eared.

During the hard winter of 1746, many of the Chillingham cattle were slaughtered from motives of charity. The *Middlewick Journal*, or *Cheshire Advertiser* of the 14th December that year had the following paragraph :—

They write from Newcastle that on Friday se'nnight (being Lord Ossulston's birthday) the Earl of Tankerville, in regard to the inclemency of the present season and great scarcity of provisions, was pleased to order a great number of the wild cattle in Chillingham Park to be slaughtered, which with a proportionable quantity of bread was on that day distributed amongst upwards of 600 poor people.

Subsequently the herd had a narrow escape from extinction. A letter from the late Lord Tankerville, in *Annals of Natural History* (1839), states that "several years since, during the early part of the lifetime of my father, the bulls in the herd had been reduced to three ; two of them fought and killed each other, and the third was discovered to be impotent ; so that the means of preserving the breed depended on the accident of some of the cows producing a bull calf," which turned out to be the case.

Chartley Park, in Staffordshire, belonging to the Earl Ferrers, has also been long celebrated for a herd of the wild white cattle with black ears. The park was formed, about 1248, out of Part of Needwood Forest ; and we are told that " some of the wild cattle of the country which had formerly roamed at large in the Forest of Needwood were driven into the park at this place (Chartley), where their breed is still preserved." The herd is occasionally mentioned in records ; but its number seems never to have averaged beyond 30. The animals are not so wild as those at Chillingham. In 1874 they numbered 25 ; and in 1877, only 20.

An old tradition connects the Chartley cattle with the singular superstition that the occurrence of a white calf in the herd is an invariable omen of death in the Chartley family. " In the year the Battle of Burton Bridge was fought, a *black* calf was born in this unique race ; and the downfall of the grand house of Ferrers happening about the same time, gave rise to the tradition, still current, that the birth of a dark-hued, or parti-coloured calf from the wild breed in Chartley Park, is a sure *omen of death* within the same year to a member of the Ferrers family. It is a noticeable coincidence, say the *Staffordshire Chronicle* of July, 1835, that a calf of this description has been born whenever a death has happened in the family of late years. The decease of the seventh Earl Ferrers, and of his countess, and of his son, Viscount Tamworth, and of his daughter, Mrs. William Jolliffe, as well as the deaths of the son and heir of the eighth earl, and of his daughter,

Lady Frances Shirley, were each preceded by the ominous birth of the fatal-hued calf. In the spring of 1835, an animal perfectly black was calved by one of this mysterious tribe, in the Park of Chartley, and the portentous event was speedily followed by the death of the Countess, the second wife of the eighth Earl Ferrers."[*]

" In Lyme Park," Cheshire, " which contains about one thousand Cheshire acres," says Hansall's *History* of that county, published in 1817, " is a herd of upwards of twenty wild cattle, similar to those in Lord Tankerville's park at Chillingham,—chiefly white with red ears. They have been in the park from time immemorial, and tradition says they are indigenous." The park was enclosed out of Macclesfield Forest, and was acquired by Sir Piers Legh from Richard II. It still remains in the possession of the Leghs, and probably the herd of cattle was introduced at the time of the grant. About 1850, the herd numbered 34 ; in 1875, only 4 ; and in 1877, there was an increase to 6. Both red and black ears have occurred in the herd. Generally the Lyme cattle have been larger than any others of the species.

Thus, as we have enumerated, herds of the white wild cattle are still preserved at two places in Scotland—Cadyow Castle and Kilmory House ; and at three places in England—Chillingham Castle, Chartley Park, and Lyme Park. But formerly, for different periods, some extending down to recent years, herds of these animals were preserved at Neworth Castle, in Cumberland ; Gisburne Park, Yorkshire ; Whalley Abbey, Lancashire ; Middleton Park, Lancashire ; Hoghton Tower, Lancashire ; Wollaton Park, Nottinghamshire ; Somerford Park,

---

[*] Ingram's *Haunted Homes and Family Traditions of Great Britain*, p. 401.

Cheshire ; Woldenby Park, Northamptonshire ; Leigh
Court, Somersetshire ; Barnard Castle, Durham ; Bishop
Auckland, Durham ; Burton Constable, Yorkshire ; and
Ewelme Park, Oxfordshire.*

Although the wild white cattle were once so numerous
in the Scottish Highlands, yet it seems ultimately to have
become a wonder to find a white ox of the domesticated
species in the north. Mrs. Grant of Laggan relates a
story which illustrates the point :—

A gentleman of no small note in Strathspey had a very remarkable animal
stolen from him. It was a white ox ; a colour rare in those northern
countries.

Mungo was not accounted a man of desperate courage ; but the white ox
being a great favourite, there was in this case no common stimulus. Mungo,
as may be supposed, had no numerous *linne na chris* [bodyguard of friends].
He took, however, his servant with him, and went to the shealing of Dry-
men, at the foot of Corryarich, where he was credibly informed his white
favourite might be found. He saw this conspicuous animal quietly grazing,
unguarded and alone ; but having thought better of the matter, or supposing
the creature looked very happy where he was, he quietly returned without
him. Being as deficient in true Highland caution as in courage, he very
innocently told when he came home, that he had seen his ox, and left it there.

The disgrace attending this failure was beyond the power of a Lowland
heart to conceive. He was all his life after, called Mungo of the White Ox ;
and to this day [1811] it is accounted very ill-bred to mention an ox of that
colour before any of his descendants. †

After the extirpation of the wild cattle and wild beasts,
we hear not only of water-bulls, but of other strange
animals in the Highlands, equally, as would appear, the
creations of imagination. What shall we say of the one

---

* For portions of information regarding the extinct and existing herds of
the white cattle, particularly in England, we are indebted to Mr. James
Edmund Harting's *British Animals Extinct within Historic Times ;* and
also to his letter in *The Field* of 6th September, 1890, in illustration of the
Earl of Tankerville's communications to that paper of 16th and 30th August
previous.

† *Essays on the Superstitions of the Highlands*, Vol. II., p. 49.

which is described by the Rev. John Grant, minister of
Kirkmichael, Banffshire, in the Old Statistical Account of
that parish ?   Among the Grampian mountains, "it is
asserted by the country people that there is a small quad-
ruped which they call *famh*.   In summer mornings it
issues from its lurking-places, emitting a kind of glutinous
matter fatal to horses, if they happen to eat of the grass
upon which it has been deposited.   It is somewhat larger
than a mole, of a brownish colour, with a large head dis-
proportionate to its body.   From this deformed appearance, and its noxious quality, the word seems to have
been transferred to denote a monster, a cruel, mischievous
person, who, in the Gaelic language, is usually called a
famh-fhear."   The same venomous creature, or one very
much akin to it, is mentioned by the author of *The
Scottish Gael* (1831) :—" A species of amphibious animal,
apparently of the rat kind, called *Beothach an' fheoir*, is
found in the eddies of the upper regions, always inhabiting the vicinity of the green patches around springs.
When a horse feeds upon the grass that has been recently
cropped by this animal, it swells, and in a short time dies,
and the flesh is found blue, as if it had been bruised or
beaten.   I believe this creature has not been hitherto
described by naturalists."*   Has any naturalist noticed it
to this day ?   But it concerns us not to press the enquiry.

Let us not forget how Virgil fables that the water of
the Campanian river, Clitumnus, rendered oxen white,
preparing them as victims " for triumphs after prosperous
wars."   The elegiac Propertius and the naturalist Pliny
also mention the same supposititious wonder.

It would seem that *Bull-baiting* was once a popular sport

* Sinclair's *Statistical Account of Scotland*, Vol. XII., p. 449 ; Logan's
Scottish Gael, Vol. II., p. 36.

in Scotland, as it was in the sister kingdom. Here is an old example :—" It happened that, in the year 1164, Ailred, the Abbot of Rievaux, was on a journey in Galloway, and was at Kirkcudbright on the festival of the saint (St. Cuthbert) from whom the place is called. On this occasion a bull of a fierce temper was brought to the church as an oblation, and was baited in the churchyard by the young clerics, notwithstanding the remonstrances of their more aged brethren, who warned the others of the danger of violating the 'peace' of the Saint within the limits of his sanctuary. The younger men persisted in their frolic, and one of them ridiculed the idea of St. Cuthbert's presence, and the consequent sanctity of the place, even though his church was one of stone—a great distinction when so many churches and chapels were still of timber. The bull, after being baited for a time, broke loose from its tormentors, and, rushing through the crowd, he attacked the young cleric who had just spoken, and gored him, without attempting to hurt any other person."* Nearly four hundred years later—in 1529—" the Provost and Bailies " of Stirling, " licensed the Deacon and Craftsmen of the Fleshers to bait ane bull on St. Cuthbert's Day, or on the Sunday next thereafter." † Such rude sports probably ceased at the Reformation.

---

* *Fourth Report of the Royal Commission on Historical Manuscripts*, p. 288.

† Extracts from the Records of the Royal Burgh of Stirling, A.D. 1519-1666.

CHAPTER II.

THE WOLVES.

Our fore-sires, peaceful, then a shepherd-race,
Did tend their flocks—or rous'd the cheering chace,
These hills and glens and wooded wilds can tell,
How many wolves, and boars, and deer then fell.
Campbell's " Grampians Desolate."

SCOTLAND has seen " good old times "—(those " ages, which," as Sismondi remarks, " can only teach us one lesson—to avert at all price their return ")—when the country people were called out periodically *en masse*, by public statute, to pursue the pleasures of the chase in its most exciting form, under pains and penalties for neglect of the summons. Many parts of Caledonia were overrun with wolves, the last surviving species of savage animals which had infested the land from the pre-historic ages. Their depredations were not always confined to the flocks and herds : frequently the sparse population of the glens had to mourn over more afflicting losses ; so that eventually the Government was forced to grapple with the evil the best way it could. The same thing had occurred both in England and Wales. According to the old chroniclers, the Principality was cleared by the annual tribute of wolves' skins, heads, or tongues imposed by King Edgar—

> Wise, potent, gracious prince !
> His subjects from their cruel foes he sav'd,
> And from rapacious savages their flocks :
> Cambria's proud kings (though with reluctance) paid
> Their tributary wolves ; head after head,
> In full account, till the woods yield no more,
> And all the ravenous race extinct is lost.

But, in fact, no such result was attained. The tribute may have thinned the numbers of the "rapacious savages"; but it did not lead to their extirpation. Long after Edgar's days Harold claimed the tribute. After the Conqueror clove his way to Harold's throne, through the carnage of Hastings, he granted the Northumbrian family of Umphraville the lands of Redesdale, to be held by the tenure of defending that part of the country from wolves and the King's foes. Other lands were held by the like tenure. Edward I. saw England suffering from the vulpine plague, and instituted vigorous repressive measures ; but a lengthened period elapsed before "the ravenous race" disappeared from the southern portion of our island.

If Hector Boece can be believed, Dornadilla, a Scottish king, who flourished two centuries before the Christian era, enacted hunting-laws, and ordained that "he that killed a wolf should have an ox for his pains ! This beast, indeed, the Scottish men, even from the beginning, used to pursue in all they might devise, because the same is such an enemy to cattle, wherein consisted the chief portion of all their wealth and substance." One of this monarch's successors, Ederus, who was contemporary with Julius Cæsar, had his "chief delight," we are told, " altogether in hunting, and keeping of hounds and greyhounds, to chase and pursue wild beasts, and namely the wolf, the herdman's foe." Another king of the same shadowy line was the debauched tyrant, Ferquhard II., who died a miserable death, in A.D. 664, from the bite of a wolf which he was hunting. Another tradition states that in 1010, when Malcolm II. was returning from Mortlach, in Moray, where he had gained a signal victory over the Danish invaders, he was attacked and chased by an immense wolf in Stochet forest.   He might have fallen a prey had not a son of Donald of the Isles flown to his assistance.   The young Islesman wrapping his plaid around his left arm and hand, thrust the muffled hand into the " gaunt grey " brute's gaping mouth, while at the same time he stabbed it to death with his dirk ; for which good service he was awarded with the Aberdeenshire lands of Skene.

But leaving fabulous history, we shall descend to times which supply authentic, albeit scattered and fragmentary, records of the prevalence of wolves throughout Scotland, and especially where the ancient forests afforded them shelter.   On the Border, in the twelfth century, the monks of Melrose were accustomed to trap the wolves on their Eskdale lands, but were prohibited from hunting the hart and hind, the boar and the roe, and also from hawking, which rights were reserved by the feudal baron who granted the Abbey the pasturage of Eskdale.   But in a following age the monks acquired the whole game-rights which had been so reserved.   In 1263 the royal park at Stirling was repaired, and a new one formed ; and twenty years afterwards, in addition to two park-keepers, there was a " hunter of wolves " at Stirling.*

In 1427 the Scottish legislature saw urgent cause to take steps for the repression of the wolf-plague.   In doing so they had precedents in the English usages of old. There was also the *Capitular* of Charlemagne, promulgated in the year 812, and one of the ordinances in which was

---

* Innes' *Sketches of Early Scotch History*, p. 103 ; and *Scotland in the Middle Ages*, p. 125.

to the effect that the "Judices" or stewards of the villas should report regularly "how many wolves each has caught, and send us their skins. And in the month of May to search and take the cubs with poison and hooks, as well as with pits and dogs." Similar action was needed in Scotland. Accordingly, the seventh Parliament of James I., which met at Perth on 1st March, 1427, commanded that "Ilk Baron, within his barony, in gangand time of the year, chase and seek the whelps of the wolves, and gar slay them. And the Baron shall give to the man that slays the wolf in his barony, and brings the Baron the head, two shillings. And when the Barons ordain to hunt and chase the wolf, the tenants shall rise with the Baron, under the pain of a wedder ilk man not rising with the Baron. And that the Barons hunt in their baronies and chase four times in the year, and as oft as any wolf be seen within the barony. And that no man seek the wolf with shot, but only in the times of hunting of them;" the last clause being evidently intended to prevent poaching of game. The edict, however, seems to have been a failure from the backwardness of the Barons to obey it. In the next reign the fourteenth Parliament of James II., in 1457, enacted "for the destruction of wolves, that in ilk country where any is, the Sheriff or the Bailie of that country shall gather the country-folk three times in the year betwixt St. Mark's Day and Lammas [25th April and 1st August], for that is the time of the whelps. And whatever he be that rises not with the Sheriff, Bailie, or Baron, within himself, shall pay unforgiven a wedder, as is contained in the auld Act made thereupon. And he that slays a wolf at any time, he shall have of ilk householder of that parish that the wolf is slain within, a penny. And if any wolf happens to come in the country that wit [intelligence] be got of, the country shall be ready, and ilk householder to hunt them, under the pain foresaid. And they that slays a wolf shall bring the head to the Sheriff, Bailie, or Baron, and he shall be debtor to the slayer for the sum foresaid. And whatsoever he be that slays a wolf, and brings the head to the Sheriff, Lord, Bailie, or Baron, he shall have six pennies."

It has been conjectured that the passing of this law originated the keeping of county kennels or packs of hounds.* The Sheriff and Bailies, for a time, would appear to have executed their commission better than the Barons, though generally in perfunctory style. " In some active instances," say the brothers Stuart, "the exertion of these statutes might have cleared local districts, and a remarkable example of success was given by a woman— Lady Margaret Lyon, Baroness to Hugh, third Lord Lovat. This lady, having been brought up in the low country, at a distance from the wolves, was probably the more affected by their neighbourhood, and caused them to be so vigorously pursued in the Aird that they were exterminated out of their principal hold in that range. According to the Wardlaw MS., 'she was a stout, bold woman, a great huntress ; she would have travelled in our hills a-foot, and perhaps out-wearied good footmen. She purged Mount Caplach of the wolves. There is a seat there called Ellig-ne-Banitearn. She lived in Phoppachy, near the sea, in a stanck-house [a house surrounded by a moat or fosse], the vestige whereof remains to this very day.' Mount Caplach is the highest range of the Aird, running parallel to the Beauly Firth, behind Moniach and Lentron. Though the place of the lady's seat is now forgotten, its existence is still remembered, and said to have been at a pass where she sat when the woods were driven

---

* Miller's *Arbroath and its Abbeys*, p. 65.

for the wolves, not only to see them killed, but to shoot at them with her own arrows. The period of her repression of the wolves is indicated by the succession of her husband to the Lordship of Lovat, which was in 1450, and it is therefore probable that the 'purging' of 'Mount Caplach' was begun soon after that date. Such partial expulsions, however, had little effect upon the general head of wolves, which, fostered by the great Highland forests, increased at intervals to an alarming extent."*

During the reigns of Jameses III. and IV., notices of the wolves are exceedingly scanty. Abbots of Abbeys being reckoned as barons, came under the law providing for the periodical chase of the wolf, and seem therefore to have kept dogs. Such, for example, was the case with the Abbot of Arbroath, who had a kennel near the Abbey.† The monks of Coupar-Angus Abbey inserted a clause in the tacks or leases of their principal tenants that they should rise to the wolf-hunt when cited so to do. Thus, in a lease of part of the lands of Innerarity, dated 24th April 1483, the tenant was taken bound to " obey the officers rising in the defence of the country to wolf, thief, and sorners." The conjunction of wolves and thieves also occurs in the old Litany of Dunkeld, which contains this prayer—" From caterans and robbers, from wolves and all wild beasts, Lord deliver us." In the Accounts of the Lord High Treasurer of Scotland, under date of 24th October, 1491, the sum of 5s. is entered as paid " to a fellow that brought the King [James IV.] two wolves, in Linlithgow ": which animals were presumably alive and intended to fight with dogs for the sport of the Court, as had they been dead, their heads only would have sufficed

---

* *Lays of the Deer Forest*, Vol. II., p. 230.
† Miller's *Arbroath and its Abbey*, p. 65.

to ensure reward. But "in the time of James V.," say the brothers Stuart, "the wolves' numbers and ravages were formidable," owing to the "clouds of forests" in various districts of the Highlands. Boece declares in his History, which was published in 1526, that "the wolves are right noisome to the tame bestial in all parts of Scotland, except a part thereof named Glenmore, in which the tame bestial gets little damage of wild bestial, especially of foxes." In the year 1528, King James was present at the great hunting in Athole (which is afterwards described), and among the scores of animals slain were wolves.

It was in the reign of Mary, Queen of Scots, however, that the wolf-plague, which had been gradually coming to a crisis, spread unexampled devastation. The wolves, when pinched with hunger, ransacked churchyards, like the ghouls of Arabian romance, feasting on the newly-buried corpses which they unearthed. Along the tract of Ederachillis, on the north-west coast of Sutherlandshire, the inhabitants were constrained to transfer the burial of their dead to the adjacent rocky islet of Handa, in the sea, where the restless surge, breaking against the precipitous cliffs, preserved the inviolability of the humble selpulchres.

> " To Handa's isle we go,
>   Our graveyard in the deep,
> Where the tombs stand all a-row,
>   Safe in that rocky keep ;
> And never a foot of man or brute
>   Disturbs our kinsmen's sleep.
>
> " On Ederachillis' shore
>   The grey wolf lies in wait,—
> Woe to the broken door,
>   Woe to the loosened gate,
> And the groping wretch whom sleety fogs
>   On the trackless moor belate.

" The lean and hungry wolf,
    With his fangs so sharp and white,
His starveling body pinched
    By the frost of a northern night,
And his pitiless eyes that scare the dark
    With their green and threatening light.

" He climbeth the guarding dyke,
    He leapeth the hurdle bars,
He steals the sheep from the pen,
    And the fish from the boat-house spars ;
And he digs the dead from out the sod,
    And gnaws them under the stars.

" Thus every grave we dug
    The hungry wolf uptore,
And every morn the sod
    Was strewn with bones and gore ;
Our mother earth had denied us rest
    On Ederachillis' shore.

" To Handa's isle we go,
    Encircled by the sea ;
A swimmer stout and strong
    The grey wolf need to be,
And a cragsman bold to scale the rocks
    If he follow where we flee.

" To Handa's isle we sail,
    Whose blood-red cliffs arise
Six hundred feet above the deep,
    And stain the lurid skies ;
Where the mainland foliage never blooms,
    And the sea-mist never dries.

" Push off for the sea-dashed grave,
    The wolf may lurk at home,
May prowl in the Diri Moir
    Till nightfall bids him roam ;
But the grave is void in the mountain kirk,
    And the dead hath crossed the foam."*

---

* Mrs. D. Ogilvy's *Book of Highland Minstrelsy*, p. 251.

Moreover, in different quarters of the country, houses of refuge or "hospitals," (*spittals*, as they were called) had to be erected, to which benighted travellers might resort for protection against the prowling rout : hence the origin of the " Spittal of Glenshee," and similar appellations in other places.

To this period may be assigned the following two traditions which we quote from a curious source, namely, *A Description of the Beauties of Edinample and Lochearn-head* (in western Perthshire)—a tract, bearing upon the title-page to have been written by a native of that district, Angus M'Diarmid by name, and which appeared in 1815, with a dedication to the Earl of Breadalbane. Angus was a thorough Child of the Mist—a trusty gillie on the moors, and a genius to boot. He appears to have acquired just sufficient knowledge of the English language to enable him to use an English dictionary, from the study of which his untutored mind formed an extraordinary style of composition. The *Description* was reprinted at Aberfeldy in 1841, and again in 1876, and is altogether unique as the production of an untaught Highlander striving to express his thoughts in literary English. A copy of the first edition apparently fell into the hands of Robert Southey, who quoted and laughed over one of its queer phrases—" men of incoherent transactions "—

In the ancient time, when the woods was more copious repletion both on the hills and on the level than it is at present, particular the oaks, which woods was a habitation to voracious wild animals, such as wolfs, which animals would slipped imperceptibly to houses, eluding observation, when the people at the field acting in their domestic management. A certain man, after being disengaged of his dies employment, upon his return to his house, he directed his eyes through the window to meet hypochondrical discovery of his youngest child on one side of the fire, and the wolf on the other side. Upon the child to have an idea of being one of his father's dogs, he uttered some merriment expression to him, as gaiety laughter, at which his father's bowels did yearn over him observing his endearment amorous child at the hazard of being swallowed up or tear in pieces by that voracious animal ; but as Providence meant otherwise for him, he drew his bow adventure, pointing to the said animal, with much anxiety how to screen his child from being injured or molested by the arrow : at which point he finished the above animal.

About the same time, the cattle of Glendochard inhabitants has been taken away by violence or pillage, by barbarous men of incoherent transactions. At that depredation, a most excellent bull break out from the force of the ravisher ; which bull shelter himself in a vacant hovel, laying a distant from the rest of the houses ; he was much troubled by one of the wolfs already mentioned, for which he was laying between the doorposts holding his head out to fence with that animal,—the said combat has been observed by two men going that way. Upon some emergent occasion, the said men came on the day following with bows and arrows, and placed themselves on the housetop where the said bull sheltered himself, waiting on the animal's coming. Upon his first discovery, the men persuaded that he was of greater stature or size than his usual circumference, they remarked two of the wolfs close together with a cross stick in their mouth. When they arrive to the bull, they yoked together on him ; the men drew their bows, and killed them on the spot. When they descended off the housetop to look at them, they found one of them blind. It was the purpose of the other to lead the blind one by the stick, to acquire his assistance to finish the said bull, being the one had practical accustomed of assaying to kill him himself.*

Up to the outbreak of the Reformation the tacks granted to tenants by the monks of Coupar-Angus Abbey embodied clauses relating to the destruction of the wolfish breed. Thus, in a lease, dated 10th September, 155—, of the lands of Mekle Forther, in Glenisla, to the Countess of Crawford and Lord Ogilvy of Airlie, her son, they are bound to " sustain and feed ane leash of hounds for tod (fox) and wolf." In another, of date 17th September, 1552, the tenants of Nether Illrik are to maintain one hound for tod and wolf. In a third, dated 16th November, same year, tenants of the Newtoun of Bellite, etc., in Glenisla, are to " maintain ane leash of good hounds, with

---

* Another version of the second tradition will be found in the *Lays of the Deer Forest*, Vol. II., pp. 232-239.

ane couple of raches (sleuth-dogs or blood-hounds), for tod and wolf, and shall be ready at all times when we charge them to pass with us or our bailies to the hunts, as we charge." A fourth lease, dated 9th March, 1557, of the Mill of Freuchy, binds the tenants to keep a leash of hounds for fox and wolf; and a fifth, dated 14th June following, of Wester Innerarity, contains a similar clause that the tenants " shall maintain and have in readiness ane leash of hounds for wolf and fox, with hunting when we or our servants please."*

But the intolerable pest eventually caused the general adoption of the most vigorous measures of repression. Extensive forests in Rannoch and Lochaber, and other quarters, were burned down to prevent harbourage of the ravagers; and so heavy was the slaughter of the latter that only a comparatively few stragglers were left skulking in the Highland wastes—the breed, however, not becoming extinct for nearly the next two centuries. As fully related in the sequel, Queen Mary visited Athole, in the month of August, 1564, and witnessed the Highland hunting on a grand scale, when five wolves were among the animals killed.

That there were wolves in the wilds of Braemar, in the early part of the seventeenth century, is attested by John Taylor, the Water Poet, who says he saw them during his memorable visit to that region in 1618. " I was the space of twelve days," he writes, " before I saw either house, corn-field, or habitation for any creature, but deer, wild horses, wolves, and such like creatures, which made me doubt that I should never have seen a house again."†

---

* *Rental Book of the Cistercian Abbey of Cupar-Angus*, Vol. II., pp. 107, 141, 176, 251, 262.

† *The Pennyles Pilgrimage* (Old Book Collector's Miscellany), p. 50.

In the year 1609, a case was before the Privy Council, in which mention was made of the pursuit of a wolf in Assynt. The Inventories of the wardrobe in Balloch (Taymouth) Castle, dating from 1598, enumerate four wolf-skins, each being probably the souvenir of a desperate chase. By the Acts of the Breadalbane Baron Courts, which were collected in 1621, each tenant was obliged to make yearly four spears for killing of the wolf; and in 1622, a case came up, concerning three cows killed by the wolf.* One of the Sutherland account-books contains an entry, in 1621, of £6 13s. 4d. being "given this year to Thomas Gordon for the killing of ane wolf, and that according to the Acts of the country." †

Various districts far apart retain each its tradition of the death of the "last wolf." In the Banffshire parish of Kirkmichael, the last wolf was said to have been slain about 1644; "yet," adds the parish minister, who gives the story, "it is probable that wolves were in Scotland for some time after that period." § Sir Ewen Cameron, the valorous chief of Lochiel, who defied Cromwell's power, and fought on Dundee's side at Killiecrankie, killed the last wolf in his country in 1680. Another was slain about the same time, in Forfarshire, by a scion of the house of Ogilvy. It is stated that about the middle of this century "two wolves, the last seen in Scotland, were chased from the wood of Trowan," near Glenturret, in western Perthshire, "and followed by their pursuers into the Highlands, where they were killed.‡ But there is a respectable tradition which goes to prove that the last

---

* *Black Book of Taymouth*

† *Second Report of the Royal Commission on Historical Manuscripts*, p. 179.

‡ Sinclair's *Statistical Account of Scotland*, vol. xii., p. 447.

§ *Statistical Account of Perthshire*, p. 731.

wolf in Scotland existed so late as 1743, in which year it was shot on the banks of the Findhorn by a famous Highland hunter, Macqueen of Pall-a'-chrocain, not many hours after it had throttled two children on the hills; and the story of its death, as told by the brothers Stuart, is worth rehearsing here. Macqueen was "of a gigantic stature, six feet seven inches in height," and "was equally remarkable for his strength, courage, and celebrity as a deer-stalker. It will not be doubted that he had the best 'long-dogs' or deer greyhounds in the country; and for their service and his own, one winter's day, about the year before-mentioned, he received a message from the Laird of Mackintosh that a large 'black beast,' supposed to be a wolf, had appeared in the glens, and the day before killed two children who, with their mother, were crossing the hills from Calder, in consequence of which a 'Tainchel,' or gathering, to drive the country was called to meet at a tryst above Fi-Giuthas, where Macqueen was invited to attend with his dogs. Pall-a'-chrocain informed himself of the place where the children had been killed, the last tracks of the wolf, and the conjectures of his haunt, and promised his assistance. In the morning the Tainchel had long assembled, and Macintosh waited with impatience, but Macqueen did not arrive; his dogs and himself were, however, auxiliaries too important to be left behind, and they continued to wait until the best of a hunter's morning was gone, when at last he appeared, and Macintosh received him with an irritable expression of disappointment. 'What was the hurry?' said Pall-a'-chrocain. Macintosh gave an indignant retort, and all present made some impatient reply. Macqueen lifted his plaid, and drew the black, bloody head of the wolf from under his arm. 'There it is for you!' said he, and tossed it on the grass in the midst of the surprised circle.

Macintosh expressed great joy and admiration, 'and gave him the land called Sean-achan for meat to his dogs.'" Macqueen died in 1797.[*]

It is well known that, in local etymology, the names of many places in England and Scotland perpetuate the memory of the wolves and of other native wild animals. In the parish of Heriot, Midlothian, "tradition reports that the glen or cleugh called the *wolf-cleugh* was once inhabited by a great wolf, which laid waste the country and attacked and destroyed every passenger. An offer was at last made that whoever would destroy this terrible animal should have as his reward a considerable portion of the territory infested by it. A man named *Dewar* at length achieved this enterprise, and called the lands by his own name."[†]

Before quitting the regions of tradition, let us recount two saintly legends relating to the wolf in Scotland, as recorded in the Breviary of Aberdeen.

St. Kentigern or Mungo, the patron saint of Glasgow, taking compassion on some husbandmen who were deprived of oxen to till their land, commanded several deer to submit to the yoke of the plough and perform the necessary labour, which they did, after which he permitted them to return to their haunts. But presently one of the submissive stags being killed by a wolf, St. Kentigern, stretching his hand towards the neighbouring wood, called on the destroyer to come forth. The wolf obeyed, and the saint yoked him to the plough along with another deer. Both animals having tilled a field of nine acres, they were set at liberty, the wolf having learned a lesson which, we may presume, he would not soon forget.

---

[*] *Lays of the Deer Forest*, vol. ii., p. 245.
[†] Forsyth's *Beauties of Scotland*, vol. i., p. 327.

The other story, similar in character, is told of St. Fillan, who, though of Irish birth, spent most of his days in the Highlands of Perthshire. Along with seven serving clerics, and also, apparently, his mother, Kentigerna, he crossed from Ireland to Scotland, his object being to visit his uncle, St. Congan, who then abode at Siracht, in the upper part of Glendeochquhy, Glendochart, or rather in Strathfillan, west of Loch Tay. Fillan arrived safely with his little party, and soon set about building a church there in honour of his uncle, the site being " divinely pointed out to him." Wondrous circumstances followed. " He completely drove away, with his little dog, a most ferocious boar which had devastated the district ; and he also converted to the faith of Christ many of the people of that place from the errors of Gentilism and idolatry. While he was building the church in the place which God had shewn him, as the oxen were being unyoked from the wains, a hungry and fierce wolf slew and ate one of them ; and in the morning, when he had no ox to take the place of that which was slain, on pouring forth prayer to God, the same wolf returned as a servant and submitted himself to the yoke with the oxen, and continued to do so till the completion of the church aforesaid, when he returned to his own nature, doing hurt to no one."*

---

* The strong family resemblance between these two stories reminds us of that of the hound Gelert, "the flower of all his race," saving the infant son of Llewellyn from a wolf, and perishing by the rash hand of his master. The scene of this legend is laid in Wales, but strangely enough the story itself is common to many countries, and seems to have originated in the East. According to Mr. Baring-Gould, "it is an introduction into Europe from India, every step of its transmission being clearly demonstrable. From the Gesta Romanorum it passed into a popular tale throughout Europe, and in different countries it was, like the Tell myth, localized and individualized. Many a Welsh story, such as those contained in the Mabinogion, are as easily traced to an Eastern origin." See *Curious Myths of the Middle Ages*, pp. 134-144.

We may conclude by remarking that although the Scottish witches, like their sisterhood in other countries, were in the habit of transforming themselves at will into the shapes of hares and cats, we hear of no Scottish warlock becoming a *loup-garou*, man-wolf, or wehr-wolf— a grisly superstition which seems never to have taken root in Scotland.

CHAPTER III.

THE DEER FOREST AND THE GROUSE MOOR.

> My heart's in the Highlands, my heart is not here ;
> My heart's in the Highlands, a-chasing the deer ;
> Chasing the wild deer, and following the roe ;
> My heart's in the Highlands wherever I go.
>
> *Old Song.*

> Now westlin' winds and slaughtering guns
> Bring autumn's pleasant weather ;
> The muircock springs, on whirring wings,
> Amang the blooming heather.
>
> *Burns.*

WAR and the chase, that " image of war, without its guilt," followed by the feast of shells and the harmonious strife of bards, filled up the chief routine of life enjoyed by the ancient tribes of Caledonia. The chase was their pastime, whence, moreover, they derived a large share of their subsistence, although they also kept domestic herds and flocks and cultivated a sprinkling of corn. From choice, as much as from necessity, the Celtic races were enthusiastic followers of Nimrod. " The desert," said Fingal, " is enough for me, with all its woods and deer !" The fame of a mighty hunter was a precious possession ; and the hunter's training inured the youth to vicissitude and peril, and moulded the future warrior. In his mythological creed, the Gael believed that the spirits of the dead found delight in pursuing ærial deer over the mountains of the silent land, and often on those of earth.   The departed "children of youth," said Ossian, "pursue deer formed of clouds, and bend their airy bow.   They still love the sport of their youth ; and mount the wind with joy."

The chase of the deer can never be robbed of its romance.   But when we speak of *stalking*, we must bear in mind that the fashion of "killing at the stalk," which requires the most patient endurance and consummate skill on the part of the hunter, is only one of several methods of slaying the deer.   Stalking, coursing, driving, and baiting, are the four modes of hunting.   The stalker creeps, steadily and unseen, to within rifle-range of his quarry.   But "hound and horn" were employed at that great hunt on Erin's green hills, when Fingal had conquered in battle, and was about to set his sails for Morven :—

" Call," said Fingal, " call my dogs, the long-bounding sons of the chase. Call white-breasted Bran, and the surly strength of Luath ! Fillan, and Ryno ; but he is not here ! My son rests on the bed of death. Fillan and Fergus ! blow the horn, that the joy of the chase may arise ; that the deer of Cromla may hear, and start at the lake of roes."

The shrill sound spreads along the wood. The sons of heathy Cromla arise. A thousand dogs fly off at once, gray-bounding through the heath. A deer fell by every dog ; three by the white-breasted Bran. He brought them, in their flight, to Fingal, that the joy of the king might be great ! One deer fell at the tomb of Ryno. The grief of Fingal returned. He saw how peaceful lay the stone of him who was the first at the chase ! "No more shalt thou rise, O my son ! to partake of the feast of Cromla. Soon will thy tomb be hid, and the grass grow rank on thy grave. The sons of the feeble shall pass along. They shall not know where the mighty lie."

With what a depth of pathos has the voice of Cona recounted those sylvan triumphs !   But we have later pictures of Highland sport which we shall pass before our readers in a succession of dissolving views.   Now-a-days, much of the slaughter in our forests is effected by the system of *driving*, the deer being forced to run the gauntlet of a narrow pass, where the sportsmen, well and securely posted, fire away as fast as their gillies can supply them with loaded rifles. It was thus, though on a far grander scale, that the *Tainchel*, or greater driving, of old was conducted. The chieftains summoned their vassals; and a wide compass of hill and wood and glen was beaten up by a *tainchel* or cordon of men, who slowly drove the deer toward the spot where the hunters lay concealed.

In the summer of 1528, King James V. made a hurried expedition to the Borders, on the pretence of hunting, but really and truly to vindicate law and justice in those turbulent regions, and "make the rush-bush keep the cow." The moss-troopers were taken by surprise, their leaders seized, and the most obnoxious consigned to the hangman. Next year the king betook himself to the Perthshire Highlands, on a peaceful excursion, accompanied by the Queen-mother and the Papal ambassador; and the magnificent reception which the royal party experienced in Athole has been detailed with great minuteness in the pages of Pitscottie :—

Upon the next summer thereafter, the King, together with his mother, and an ambassador of the Pope's, who was in Scotland for the time, went all together to Athole to the hunts. The Earl of Athole hearing of his coming, made great and gorgeous provision for him in all things pertaining to a prince, that he was as well cared for in all things as if he had been in one of his own palaces. For this noble Earl of Athole caused make ane curious palace to the King, his mother, and the ambassador, whereby they were as well eased as if they had been in any palace either of Scotland or England, and equivalent for the time of their hunting; which was biggit in the middle of a green meadow, and the walls thereof was of green timber, woven with birks, and biggit in four quarters, as if it had been a palace, and in every quarter a round like a block-house, which were lofted and joisted three house height; the floor was laid with green earth, and strewed with such flowers as grow in the meadow, that no man knew whereon he gade, but as he had been in a green garden. Farther, there was two great rounds on every side of the yett, and a great portcullis of tree falling down as it had been a barrace yett, with a great drawbridge, and a foussie of sixteen feet deep and thirty feet broad of water. This palace was hung with fine tapestry within, and well lighted in all necessary parts with glass windows.

The King was very well entertained in this wilderness the space of three days, with all such delicious and sumptuous meats as was to be had in Scotland, for fleshes, fishes, and all kinds of fine wine, and spices, requisite for a prince. Farther, there was no fishes that could live in fresh waters, but were there swimming in the foussie about the palace.

[That is to say all kind of drink, as ale, beer, wine, both white and claret, Malvoisie, Muscadel, elegant Hippocras, and aquavitæ. Farther, there was of meats—wheat-bread, main-bread, and gingerbread, with fleshes beef and mutton, lamb, veal, and venison, goose, gryce (pigs), capon, cunning (rabbits), crane, swan, partridge, plover, duck, drake, brissel-cock (turkey-cock) and paunies (peacocks), blackcock and moorfowl, capercailzies. And also the stanks (fosses or ditches full of water) that were round about the palace, were full of all delicate fishes, as salmon, trouts, perches, pikes, eels, and all other kind of delicate fishes that could be gotten in fresh water, and were all ready for the banquet. Syne were there proper stewards, cunning bakers, excellent cooks, and potingars (apothecaries) with confections and drugs for their desserts.]

It is said, by the space of thir three days that his grace was there, the Earl of Athole was every day one thousand pounds of expenses. This Pope's Ambassador, seeing so great a triumph in a wilderness, where there was no town near by twenty miles, he thought it a great marvel that such a thing should be in Scotland : that is, so court-like and delicious entertainment in the Highlands of Scotland, where he saw nothing but woods and wilderness. But most of all, this Ambassador, when the King was coming back from the hunts, marvelled to see the Highlanders set all this palace on fire, that the King and the Ambassador might see it. Then the Ambassador said to the King, "I marvel, sir, you let burn yon palace wherein you were so well eased." The King answered, "It is the use of our Highlandmen that, be they never so well lodged all the night, they will burn the same on the morn." This being done, the King returned to Dunkeld that night, and on the morn to St. Johnstoun (Perth). It is said, at this time, in Athole and Strathardle bounds, there was slain thirty score of hart and hind, with other small beasts, such as roe and roebuck, wolf, fox, and wild cats, etc.*

---

* *The Cronicles of Scotland.* By Robert Lindsay of Pitscottie. Edited by J. Graham Dalyell. Vol. ii., p. 343. The passage within brackets is from a later MS. than that adopted by Mr. Dalyell, and bears, in his opinion, strong evidence of interpolation.

Probably the fame of this right royal hunting induced the fair and unfortunate daughter of King James to honour Athole with her presence in 1564, when she made a progress of two months through her northern dominions. It has been said by one of Mary's biographers (Sheriff Glassford Bell) that the years 1563 and 1564 were " the quietest and the happiest she spent in Scotland," for all political troubles were dispelled, and she was looking forward to a happy union and a peaceful and gracious reign. " Love was young, and Darnley kind." She was at Perth in May, 1564, and about the beginning of August she reached Athole, and witnessed the glories of the *tainchel* in the wilds of Glen Tilt. The exciting scene has been described, in stately Latin, by a gentleman of her train—William Barclay, the scion of a good family in Aberdeenshire. He was then three and twenty, and a Roman Catholic. He continued attached to the Court till the Queen's captivity in England, when he crossed to France, and applied himself to the study of civil law. He subsequently married a French lady, and lived till 1605, when he died Professor of Civil Law in the University of Angers. He was the father of the erratic author of *Argenis*, which Cowper, the poet, declared to be " the most amusing romance that ever was written." The account of the Athole hunting is contained in one of the Civilian's Latin works—*De Regno et Regali Potestate adversus Monarchomachos*—(a treatise against Buchanan and his Republican school) and has been translated by Mr. Pennant :—

" I had a sight of a very extraordinary sport. In the year 1563 [a mistake for 1564], the Earl of Athol, a prince of the blood-royal, had, with much trouble, and vast expence, provided a hunting-match for the entertainment of our illustrious and most gracious Queen. Our people call this a royal hunting. I was then a young man, and was present on that occasion. Two thousand Highlanders were employed to drive to the hunting-ground all the deer from the woods and hills of Athol, Badenoch, Marr, Murray, and the countries about. As these Highlanders use a light dress, and are very swift of foot, they went up and down so nimbly, that, in less than two months' time, they brought together two thousand red deer, besides roes and fallow deer. The Queen, the great men, and a number of others were in a glen, or narrow valley, where all these deer were brought before them; believe me, the whole body moved forward in something like battle order. This body still strikes me, and ever will strike me; for they had a leader whom they followed close wherever he moved. This leader was a very fine stag, with a very high head. The sight delighted the Queen very much, but she soon had cause for fear, upon the Earl (who had been from his earliest years accustomed to such sights) addressing her thus : ' Do you observe that stag who is foremost of the herd ? There is danger from that stag; for if either fear or rage should force him from the ridge of that hill, let every one look to himself, for none of us will be out of the way of harm, as the rest will all follow this one; and having thrown us under foot, they will open a passage to the hill behind us.' What happened a moment after confirmed this opinion; for the Queen ordered one of the best dogs to be let loose upon a wolf;[*] this the dog pursues—the leading stag was frightened—he flies by the same way he had come there—the rest rush after him where the thickest body of the Highlanders was. They had nothing for it but to throw themselves flat on the heath, and to allow the deer to pass over them. It was told the Queen that several of the Highlanders had been wounded, and that two or three had been killed outright; and the whole body of deer had got off, had not the Highlanders, by their skill in hunting, fallen upon a stratagem to cut off the rear from the main body. It was of those that had been separated, that the Queen's dogs, and those of the nobility, made slaughter. There was killed that day three hundred and sixty deer, with five wolves, and some roes."

After the hunt, the Queen is said to have presided over a competition of Highland harpers, when she awarded the prize to the Lady Beatrix Gardyn, of Banchory, Aberdeenshire. A descendant of this fair minstrel married into the Robertson family of Lude, and brought with her the harp gifted on the above occasion.

There were spacious hunting-grounds on the Scottish

---

[*] Mr. Pennant erroneously renders it, "on one of the deer;" but the words of the original are—"*Laxatus enim reginæ jussu, atque immissus in lupum, insignis admodum ac ferox canis.*"

Border, to which our kings frequently resorted " to chase
the deer with hound and horn ;" but as might be ex-
pected, the laws against poaching were ill-observed in that
turbulent region. Two years after the Queen's hunt in
Athole, there was found a great scarcity of deer on the
Border for the royal sport ; and the Scottish Privy
Council, sitting at Rodono, on the 16th August, 1566,
passed an ordinance setting forth that despite the Acts of
Parliament against the unlawful shooting of deer, the
latter were so " halelie (wholly) destroyed, that our
sovereigns (Mary and her consort, Darnley) can get no
pastime of hunting now when their highnesses is purposely
repaired in this country (the Border land) to that effect ;"
and therefore commanding all and sundry, the lieges, to
abstain from breach of the laws in future. Again, the
Council, on 27th March, 1576, understanding that, "as the
deer within the bounds of Meggatland, Eskdale-muir, and
other bounds west the borders of this realm, where our
Sovereign Lord's progenitors "—for the hapless Mary was
now dethroned and a captive—" had wont to have their
chief pastime of hunting, are not only slain by guns with
Scotsmen, but also by the hunting of Englishmen, brought
and conveyed in to the said parts in arms by Scotsmen
inhabiting the Borders, without conduct or licence of our
Sovereign Lord or his Wardens, and hunting by Scotsmen
themselves in forbidden time,"—a strict prohibition of
such practices was issued, and it was ordained that none
such hunt at any time between Fastren's Even (Shrove-
tide) and Midsummer. Such fulminations evidently were
spent in air ; and we may only further notice that on 6th
March, 1600, the King and Council denounced deer-
poaching in the Highlands and on the Borders, and
enacted that all defaulters should be " held to make payment of the sum of three hundred merks for every deer so

to be shot and slain, the one half to his Majesty, and the other half to the dilater and avower." *

Half-a-century after Queen Mary's visit to Athole, a votary of literature, better known than the learned Civilian, journeyed from England to the north, and joined in the Highland sport of hunting the deer. Who has not heard of the *Water-Poet*—John Taylor, the poetic Waterman of the Thames?

> And did you ne'er hear of a jolly young waterman,
>   Who at Blackfriars' Bridge used for to ply ?
> He feather'd his oars with such skill and dexterity,
>   Winning each heart, and delighting each eye.

In 1618—the year when Ben Jonson came down to meet his friend Drummond, amid the classic shades of Hawthornden—our Water Poet conceived the project of travelling to Scotland on foot, and viewing the country, without taking a penny in his purse (though he was by no means scant of cash), and trusting to the kindness of friends by the way ! It looked *prima facie* a foolhardy enterprise enough—an open-eyed, deliberate tempting of Providence, inasmuch as the poverty of Scotland was proverbial, and the south was overrun with needy Scots in quest of fortune which their own country had denied them. Nevertheless, John was not reckoning without his host. His fame was widely known : he had influential patrons in Scotland—notably Sir William Murray of Abercairney, for one, on whose hospitality he could rely.

> Then, farewell, my trim-built wherry,
>   Oars, and coat, and badge, farewell.

John left London on the 14th of July, making his way out of the city by easy stages from tavern to tavern,

---

* Register of the Privy Council of Scotland, vol. I., p. 477 ; vol. II., p. 506 ; vol. VI., pp. 90, 91.

where " good fellows trooping " insisted on drinking with
him the parting bowl.   At the Bell Inn, beyond Alders-
gate he procured a stout nag to carry his " provant " or
provisions, and then, "well rigged and ballasted, both with
beer and wine," set forth on his "jaunt."   In all the
English towns and villages through which he passed he
was received with open doors and open arms and plenty
of good cheer.   Crossing the Border, he still met the best
of treatment, though " not carrying any money," and
" neither begging, borrowing, or asking meate, drinke, or
lodging."   In due time he arrived at Perth : where, says
he, " mine host told me that the Earl of *Mar*, and Sir
William Murray of *Abercairney* were gone to the great
hunting to the *Brae* of *Mar;* but if I made haste I might
perhaps find them at a town called *Brekin* or *Brechin*, two
and thirty miles from Saint *Johnstone*, whereupon I took
a guide to *Brechin* the next day, but before I came, my
lord was gone from thence four days."

Although thus baulked, and with the Grampians frown-
ing before him, our undaunted poet determined to cross
the mountains to Braemar.   The difficulties and dangers
of the journey might have appalled a less adventurous
Southron ; but John girded up his loins, and trudged on
undismayed.   Safely he reached Braemar Castle, where
he was warmly welcomed by the Earl of Mar, and Abercairney, and the other noblemen and gentlemen, with their
ladies, who were there assembled.   The account of his
tour, which he afterwards wrote and published under the
title of *The Pennyles Pilgrimage, or, The Money-lesse
perambulation*, is a quaint melange of rough-spun verse
and sturdy prose, depicting with much fidelity the Highland gathering and sport.   Of the Highlanders, he says :

Their habit is shoes with but one sole apiece ; stockings (which they call
short hose) made of a warm stuff of divers colours, which they call tartan :

as for breeches, many of them, nor their forefathers, never wore any, but a jerkin of the same stuff that their hose is of, their garters being bands or wreaths of hay or straw, with a plaid about their shoulders, which is a mantle of divers colours, of much finer and lighter stuff than their hose, with blue flat caps on their heads, a handkerchief knit with two knots about their neck ; and thus are they attired.   Now their weapons are long bows and forked arrows, swords and targets, harquebusses, muskets, dirks, and Lochaber axes.   With these arms I found many of them armed for the hunting.   As for their attire, any man of what degree soever that comes amongst them, must not disdain to wear it ; for if they do, then they will disdain to hunt, or willingly to bring in their dogs ; but if men be kind unto them, and be in their habit ; then are they conquered with kindness, and the sport will be plentiful.   This was the reason that I found so many noblemen and gentlemen in those shapes.

Having been "put into that shape" himself—that is, having donned the garb of old Gaul, John accompanied the party to the hunting-ground, which is thought to have been the district around the skirts of Ben Muicdhui.

I was the space of twelve days after, before I saw either house, corn-field, or habitation for any creature, but deer, wild horses, wolves, and such like creatures, which made me doubt that I should never have seen a house again.

Thus the first day we travelled eight miles, where were small cottages built on purpose to lodge in, which they call Lonchards, I thank my good Lord *Erskine*, he commanded that I should always be lodged in his lodging, the kitchen being always on the side of a bank, many kettles and pots boiling, and many spits turning and winding, with great variety of cheer : as venison baked, sodden, roast, and stewed beef, mutton, goats, kid, hares, fresh salmon, pigeons, hen, capons, chickens, partridge, moor-coots, heath-cocks, capercailzies, and termagants [ptarmigans] ; good ale, sack, white, and claret, tent [or Alicante] with most potent *aquavitæ*.

All these, and more than these we had continually, in superfluous abund-ance, caught by Falconers, Fowlers, Fishers, and brought by my Lord's tenants and purveyors to victual our camp, which consisted of fourteen or fifteen hundred men and horses ; the manner of the hunting is this : five or six hundred men do rise early in the morning, and they do disperse them-selves divers ways, and seven, eight, or ten miles compass, they do bring or chase in the deer in many herds (two, three, or four hundred in a herd) to such or such a place, as the Nobleman shall appoint them ; then when day is come, the Lords and gentlemen of their companies do ride or go to the

said places, sometimes wading up to their middles through bournes and
rivers: and then: they being come to the place, do lie down on the ground,
till those foresaid scouts, which are called the Tinchel, do bring down the
deer: but as the proverb says of a bad cook, so these Tinchel men do lick
their own fingers; for besides their bows and arrows, which they carry with
them, we can hear now and then a harquebuss or a musket go off, which
they do seldom discharge in vain. Then after we had stayed there three
hours or thereabouts, we might perceive the deer appear on the hills round
about us, (their heads making a show like a wood) which being followed
close by the Tinchel are chased down into the valley where we lay; then
all the valley on each side being waylaid with a hundred couple of strong
Irish grey-hounds, they are let loose as the occasion serves upon the herd of
deer, so that with dogs, guns, arrows, dirks, and daggers, in the space of
two hours, fourscore fat deer were slain, which after are disposed of some
one way, and some another, twenty and thirty miles, and more than enough
left for us to make merry withal at our rendesvous.

He "liked the sport so well" that he composed a couple
of sonnets in its praise, one of which we shall quote :—

> If sport like this can on the mountains be,
> Where *Phœbus* flames can never melt the snow,
> Then let who list delight in vales below,
> Sky-kissing mountains pleasure are for me :
> What braver objects can man's eyesight see,
> Than noble, worshipful, and worthy wights,
> As if they were prepared for sundry fights,
> Yet all in sweet society agree ?
> Through heather, moss, 'mongst frogs, and bogs, and fogs,
> 'Mongst craggy cliffs, and thunder-battered hills,
> Hares, hinds, bucks, roes, are chased by men and dogs,
> Where two hours hunting fourscore fat deer kills.
> Lowland, your sports are low as is your seat,
> The Highland games and minds are high and great.

When the hunters returned nightly to their lodgings,
" there was much baking, boiling, roasting, and stewing,
as if Cook Ruffian had been there to have scalded the
devil in his feathers; and after supper a fire of firwood as
high as an indifferent Maypole." Our traveller then
relates that having spent certain days at this " unmatch-

able hunting," he accompanied the party "to the next county, called Badenoch, belonging to the Earl of Enzie, where, having much sport and entertainment as we formerly had, after four or five days' pastime, we took leave of hunting for that year." He was afterwards taken to Balloch Castle (Castle Grant) and Tarnaway, and thence returned by Elgin to the Lowlands. At Leith he found his "long approved and assured good friend, Master Benjamin Jonson," who gave him "a piece of gold or two, and twenty shillings to drink his health in England :" and on Thursday morning, the fifteenth of October, the poetic waterman reached his own house in London. Next year he issued *A Kicksey Winsey: or, A Lerry Come Twang*, wherein he "satyrically suited 800 of his bad debtors," or subscribers, " that would not pay him for his return of his journey from Scotland;" but whether this effusion produced a satisfactory result we cannot tell.

During the time of the Commonwealth, a grand stag-hunting took place in the forest of Monar, in Glen Strath-farar, Inverness-shire, conducted by the Earl of Seaforth and the Master and Tutor of Lovat. This was in 1655. The party, says a manuscript of the period, "got sight of six or seven hundred deers, and sport of hunting" for four days, "fitter for kings than country gentlemen": and " two Englishmen who were in company, declared that in all their travels they never had such brave divertisement ; and if they should relate it in England it would be concluded mere rant and incredible." *

Another great hunting was held at Braemar, in August 1715. It was attended by the leaders of the Jacobite party in Scotland, with more than a thousand followers ; and there the Earl of Mar arranged his insurrection in favour of the Chevalier de St. George.

---

* Anderson's *Guide to the Highlands*, 1863 ; p. 595.

Captain Burt, the English Officer of Engineers, who was in the Highlands, under General Wade, about 1730, is believed to have written the *Letters from a Gentleman in the North of Scotland*, which contain so lively a delineation of Highland life and manners ; and the *Tainchel*-hunting (from personal experience or otherwise) comes under his pen. But he makes no mention of dogs being employed, conceiving, in fact, that if they were kept, "their cry in those open hills would soon fright all the deer out of that part of the country ; " for the barking of an English hound, at night, in one of the military barracks, "was loudly complained of by some of the lairds, as being prejudicial to their estates." He thus speaks of the sport :

When a solemn hunting is resolved on, for the entertainment of relations and friends, the haunt of the deer being known, a number of the vassals are summoned, who readily obey by inclination ; and are, besides, obliged by the tenure of their lands, of which one article is, that they shall attend the *master* at his huntings. This, I think, was part of the ancient vassalage in England.

The chief convenes what numbers he thinks fit, according to the strength of his clan : perhaps three or four hundred. With these he surrounds the hill, and as they advance upwards, the deer flies at the sight of them, first of one side, then of another ; and they still, as they mount, get into closer order, till, in the end, he is enclosed by them in a small circle, and there they hack him down with their broad-swords. And they generally do it so dexterously, as to preserve the hide entire.

If the chase be in a wood, which is mostly upon the declivity of a rocky hill, the tenants spread themselves as much as they can, in a rank extending upwards ; and march, or, rather, crawl forward with a hideous yell. Thus they drive everything before them, while the laird and his friends are waiting at the farther end with their guns to shoot the deer. But it is difficult to force the roes out of their cover ; insomuch that when they come into the light, they sometimes turn back upon the huntsmen, and are taken alive.[*]

Barclay's (the Civilian) account of Queen Mary's hunting mentions fallow-deer ; but this must be an anachronism,

---

[*] Letters, edited by R. Jamieson, vol. II., pp. 67-70.

because it seems clearly established that that species was
not known in Scotland till the time of James VI., who,
indeed, is said to have brought the first specimens with
him when he returned home from Denmark along with
his consort Anne, the Danish Princess ; and the breed
was subsequently carried into England.   The famous
ancestor of the Breadalbane family, Black Duncan of the
Cowl, who built his castle of Balloch where Taymouth
Castle now stands, was a great rural improver, and
eagerly assisted in the introduction of fallow-deer into
Scotland.   This was in the beginning of the seventeenth
century.   In 1614 he leased the Isle of Inchesaile from
the Earl of Argyll, and next year "put fallow deir and
cunnyngis" therein.   Here a fact worth noting suggests
itself.   About the year 1850 a number of fallow-deer
broke out of the parks at Taymouth Castle, and spread
themselves over all the neighbourhood.   Some descended
to the hills around Dunkeld and Birnam, where they grew
quite wild, and became the pest of the country by
ravaging kitchen-gardens, potato-pits, and the like.   They
were systematically shot down as opportunities offered,
until their extermination was supposed to be complete.
But this was not so ; for, in the summer of 1870, a solitary
survivor—a last year's fawn of the fallow breed—appeared
in a grass park, within a mile of Birnam, where it was
seen grazing along with a flock of sheep and lambs !
The peculiarity of its companionship ensured this last of
its race against powder and shot during the time it herded
with the fleecy denizens of the fold ; but it ultimately
disappeared, and its fate is unknown.

It has been supposed, though on slender grounds, that
the ancient Scots domesticated a species of deer, just as
the Laplanders domesticated the reindeer.   A large
stag's horn, found in Blairdrummond Moss, shewed a

circular perforation, into which was fitted a piece of wood
—but for what purpose?*

Sir Robert Gordon, the Sutherland genealogist, asserts
that in the mountain of Arkel, in the forest of Dirimore,
Sutherlandshire, there was a peculiar sort of deer, which
had forked tails, three inches long, whereby they were
easily known from any others.

In the year 1622 there was a *White Hind* about
Corrichiba, in the country of Breadalbane, which King
James VI. heard of, and was exceedingly anxious to
secure for the sake of its curiosity. He was at the pains
to send down from England one of his foresters named
Scandoner, and some others, with the following letter to
Black Duncan of the Cowl:—

"To our trusty and well-beloved Sir Duncan Campbell of Glenurchy,
Knight.

"JAMES R.—Trusty and well-beloved, We greet you well. Having
understood that there is in your bounds a white hind, we have sent this
bearer, one of our servants, to take and transport her hither unto us; and
because that country is altogether unknown to him, we have thought good
hereby to recommend him to you most earnestly, requiring you to assist him
and cause him to be furnished with all things necessary, as well for taking
of the said hind as for his own entertainment; and nothing doubting of your
best endeavour for accomplishing of this our pleasure, we bid you farewell.
Given at our manor of Theobalds, the 13th day of January, 1622."

It is recorded that "the said Englishmen saw the hind
in Corrichiba on 22nd February, 1622," but they did not
succeed in taking it, and so had to return empty-handed.
The King was so anxious about this *lusus naturæ*, that on
learning his servants' ill-luck, he directed Sir Patrick
Murray to write another letter to Black Duncan:—

"To my honourable Chief, the Laird of Glenorchey, these.

"NOBLE CHIEF.—I have received from the Earl of Mar a packet of
letters concerning the taking of this troublesome white hind of yours, and

---

* Logan's *Scottish Gael*, vol. II., p. 53.

has delivered and read them to his Majesty, he being not well of a pain in his legs, I dare not say the gout.   His Majesty is well pleased with you for the care you have had to further his Majesty's desire in all things concerning this business of taking this deer, and seeing his Majesty finds by Scandoner's own letters and all yours that it is a hard matter either to take her or carry her to the sea, by reason of the difficulty and hardness of the place and hard time of the year ; and finding also by his Majesty's own experience that if she cannot be taken before May or June, being so late in the year, that if she prove with calf may endanger her own life and her calf also, his Majesty's pleasure is that she shall not be stirred this year, and that his Majesty will think of some other course before the next year for the better effecting of his desires ; and his Majesty has commanded me to write unto the Earl of Mar to send unto all those that borders or marches with Corrichiba that none presume to stir her under his Majesty's highest displeasure.   And because his Majesty will try what Scandoner can do by his art, he has written his letters to the Earl of Perth, that he may make trial in Glenartney for taking of some deer and roes now presently, that he may, by his trial there, judge what he can do hereafter in Corrichiba.   I have done you the best offices that lies in my power to his Majesty, both in this and in all other things that shall either touch or concern you, as I am bound in duty of blood to do.   Thus, with the remembrance of my true love to yourself and all yours, I rest your very assured friend and kinsman to serve you.

" P. Murray.

"Theobalds Park, the 9 of March, 1622."

The King himself wrote Black Duncan a special letter of thanks in the following July.*   So far as appears, however, the white hind never fell into the toils of the hunters, but wandered her time among the solitudes of her native wilds—a creature of marvel and superstitious mystery, and beautiful in her snowy purity as the white doe of Rylstone.

A sad misfortune which befel Abbot, Archbishop of Canterbury, while following the chase in Lord Zouch's park at Harringworth, in Hampshire, shows that deer-

---

* Innes' *Sketches of Early Scottish History*, pp. 516-518.   As with the previous extract from Pitscottie, so with the above Letters, we have modernised the old orthography.

hunters were late in abandoning the bow.   It was the
24th of July, 1622.   The prelate was on horseback, and
armed with the cross-bow.   As the deer darted past him,
he discharged a barbed arrow, but (like the bolt that slew
the Red King), it flew wide, and lodged in the left arm of
one of the park-keepers named Peter Hawkins, and the
man died in less than an hour.   The event has no parallel
in the ecclesiastical annals of England.   The Archbishop
was deeply grieved ; and it is said that, throughout the
remainder of his life, he observed a monthly fast on the
day of the week on which his hand had been thus stained
with blood.   He also settled a pension of twenty pounds
on the keeper's widow.   In Scotland, after the middle of
last century, a Highland poacher committed great depredations in the forests with his bow and arrows, and was
probably the last who so used such weapons.   He was
seized *red-hand*, and brought before the Duke of Athole,
who, hearing him vaunt of his skill in archery, pointed to
a stag, and desired him to shoot it through the off eye.
The Highlander giving a particular whistle, the animal
looked round, and immediately received an arrow in the
intended spot.*

The extreme longevity of the deer was once popularly
credited.   " Thrice the age of a man is that of a deer,"
said the Gaelic adage.   But it is now ascertained that
twenty years comprise the utmost term of life enjoyed by
the species.   That deer are keenly susceptible of the
charms of music has also been asserted.   Waller, the poet,
alludes to this notion in his Farewell Verses to Dorothy
—" At Penshurst "—

> " While in this park I sing, the list'ning deer
>   Attend my passion, and forget to fear."

* * *

* *English Forests and Forest Trees*, p. 273.   Logan's *Scottish Gael*, vol.
II., p. 45.

And again in his lines " Of my Lady Isabella," as she
played on a lute—

> " Here Love takes stand, and while she charms the ear,
> Empties his quiver on the listening deer."

Playford relates, in his *Introduction to Music*, that once he
" met on the road near Royston, a herd of about twenty
stags, following a bagpipe and violin, which, while the
music played, went forward, when it ceased they all stood
still, and in this manner they were brought out of Yorkshire to Hampton Court!"   Ought not the Highland
deer to be slaves of the bagpipe music—unless, in their
case, familiarity begets contempt?

We will not enter upon the tedious subject of the old
laws concerning foresting, or turn up the antiquated
pages of the Scottish *Leges Forestarum*, a disputable compilation.   Enough here to say, with the Duke of Argyll—
" It is a great blunder to suppose that deer forests are a
modern invention in the Highlands.   The high money
value of these forests is new, but nothing else.   The truth
is that an area enormously larger than now was formerly
occupied by nothing but deer." *   In 1584, James VI.
appointed a keeper of the royal forests of Braemar,
Cromar, and Strathdee, who was empowered " to cause
train (preserve) the said woods, forests, and muirs, and to
search and seek, take and apprehend all and whatsoever
persons hunting or repairing therein, with bows, culverins
(guns) or nets, or any other instrument meet and convenient for the destruction of the deer and the muirfowls
. . . and to present these persons to the justice,
sheriff, or any other ordinary judge, to be punished conform to the laws of this realm." †   A century afterwards—

---

* *Scotland as it was and as it is.*   Second edition, p. 204.
† *Collectanea de rebus Albanicis.*   (Iona Club.)   Vol. I., p. 189.

in 1687—the Earl of Breadalbane appointed a forester for the south side of Corrichiba (once the haunt of the *white hind*), who was bound " to stop all passengers travelling through it with guns ; to free himself, his family, and any who lodged with him, of eating venison, except the umbles and entrails of such as shall be killed for the Earl's use ; to kill in seasonable time of the year, that is, from Midsummer to Hallowmas, the number of sixteen deer, to be sent to the officer of Finlarg, the chamberlain of Glenurchy detaining from him a boll of meal for every deer he is short of the number." *

From the deer forests we now pass to the moors. During the last half century or more the annual rents of the moors have risen so much as to form a most important element in the value of Highland estates. High as are the rents, it is not impossible in good seasons, since the extension of railways has afforded facilities for the speedy conveyance of game to the southern markets, that moor lessees may manage to reimburse themselves. The recurrence of bad seasons is now more than ever to be dreaded ; for, of recent times, the moors have been frequently devastated by what is called the " Grouse disease," the cause of which seems as yet to have eluded discovery. Early in the present century, we find the distemper attracting attention. The *Sporting Magazine* for October, 1817, says :—

An extraordinary disease has lately spread more havoc among the grouse in the North of Scotland, than the double-barrelled guns of the numerous sportsmen. The birds are found dead on the hills in great numbers, and in a state of extenuation, as if they had perished from hunger.

In the same magazine for August, 1819, appeared a notice from an Edinburgh paper :—

* *Black Book of Taymouth*, p. 427.

A correspondent in the Highlands observes, that this season some un-accountable pestilential disease has attacked the moor game in some of the northern counties, and which has destroyed a very great number of them ; their smell is so loathsome and offensive that their common enemies, viz., the wild birds and collie dogs, will not approach them.

The disease broke out in 1828, when the *Greenock Advertiser* had the following remarks :—

Having heard a great deal about a destructive disease spreading devasta-tion among the moor game of this district, we have taken some trouble to inquire into the truth of the report, and having ascertained it to be correct, we afterwards caused some inquiries to be made into the nature of the malady. From Mr. Wallace, of Kelly, a well-known adept in sporting matters in this immediate neighbourhood, several grouse, in a state of com-plete emaciation, were sent to town. These were carefully dissected by one of our medical friends, and the disease found in all of them to be tape-worm. It is quite astonishing to observe the extent to which this disease can exist in the feathered tribe before causing death.

Mr. Wallace attributes this dreadful malady, and the occasional scarcity or plentifulness of game generally, to one and the same cause, viz., a con-tinuance of damp and wet weather, with little sunshine, during the spring and summer months ; or, as his own words gave it—" Game, like wheat, will abound in proportion to the heat of the season, and the continued brilliancy of the sun." Mr. Wallace is aware that this opinion is at variance with the generally received one of the older sportsmen ; but a laborious series of observations made by himself have confirmed him in the accuracy of the remark. The sporting men of other days affirmed that dry summers cause death to game for want of water : Mr. Wallace thinks that with warm nights there cannot be too much sun or too little rain, and this for any species of game in the west of Scotland, for in such weather heavy dews never fail to supply their wants.

To suggest a cure for this evil (when we have to do with the untamed and uncontrolled tenants of the moors) is obviously next to impossible. The disease can be cured in domesticated animals, it is true ; and in small pre-serves, perhaps, some means might be taken to induce the birds to eat of food imbued with so much turpentine, or other substance known to be destructive to the worms, as to effect their removal.

As to the origin of the disease, and also whether there are not two of distinct types, opinions are still at variance. The whole question is beset with difficulties; but probably the disease may be traced to atmospheric influences, or, in other words, exceptional and protracted disturbances of the due temperature of seasons acting prejudicially on the natural food of the grouse. This theory obtains respectable support. Dr. Thomas Cobbold, of London, attributes the distemper to intestinal irritation caused by the presence of parasites—tape-worms and thread-worms. Writers of some experience lay much to account of the heather-blight ; but hold that " the crying evil " is the overstocking of moors with sheep, which deprive the grouse to an increasing extent of their natural food, the heather. For ourselves, we cannot venture to speak authoritatively on the subject : but, doubtless with farther painstaking observation, conducted irrespective of all pre-conceived notions, the real root of the evil will be reached, and a remedy found.

CHAPTER IV.

FOX-HUNTING.

> With hunts up, with hunts up,
>   It is now perfect day.
>   .   .   .   .
> Ane cursed fox lay hid in rocks
>   This lang and mony a day,
> Devouring sheep ; while he micht creep,
>   Nane might him schape away.
>   *Wedderburne's Ballads.*

IT has been truly remarked that " in Scotland, where, from the character of the country, fox-hunting is often impossible, it never has become a national sport to the same extent as in England." At an early period the Scots did not reckon the fox among their beasts of chase, and neither did the English. For other sport was afforded by the pathless forests, the brown moors, the bosky glens, and heathy mountain of the north, where the "mighty hunters" of old, who contended with the wild white bull, the wolf, and the boar, and revelled in the chase of the deer, disdained to pursue the mean and cowardly fox—the *madadh ruadh*, the red dog, as it was called in the language of the hills. By skill in hunting, the young chief of a clan gave the first proof of capacity to head his tribe ; but the red dog was not the quarry against which he bent his adolescent energies.

The fox, which abounded in the country, proving most destructive to flocks and domestic poultry, was counted as vermin, and was trapped and otherwise distroyed by the rural population who suffered severely from its ravages. Hear what Roderick Dhu said—

> " Though the beast of game
> The privilege of chase may claim,
> Though space and law the stag we lend,
> Ere hound we slip, or bow we bend,
> Who ever reck'd, where, how, or when,
> The prowling fox was trapp'd or slain ? "

Unlike the wolf, however, the fox never had the honour of being denounced by statute, but in various quarters dogs were kept specially for its extirpation. Thus, for example, the Register of Tacks of the Abbey of Cupar-Angus, which had extensive domains in Glenisla, contains leases, dated between 1539 and 1559, in which the larger tacksmen were severally held bound to maintain and feed " a leash of good hounds, with a couple of raches (sleuth-dogs) for tod (fox) and wolf, and shall be ready at all times when we (the abbot and convent) charge them to pass with us or our baillies to the hunts ;" and the smaller tenants were in like manner bound to keep " one hound for tod and wolf."*

Hector Boece, in his *History*, tells a marvellous story of how the inhabitants of Glenmore (in the shires of Inverness and Moray) protected their fowls against the wily plunderers. " The wolves," he says, " are right noisome to the tame bestial in all parts of Scotland, except one part thereof, named Glenmore ; in which the tame bestial get little damage of wild bestial, especially of tods. For each house nourishes a young tod certain days, and mixes

---

* *Rental Book of the Cistercian Abbey of Cupar-Angus.* (Grampian Club). Vol. II., pp. 107, 141, 176, 251, 262.

the flesh thereof, after it be slain, with such meat as they give to their fowls or other small beasts, and so many as eat of this meat are preserved two months after from any damage by the tods, for tods will taste no flesh that tastes of their own kind ; and be there but one beast or fowl that has not tasted of this meat, the tod will chase it out among a thousand." No comment on this mode of protection is needful.

At what period the chase of the fox came in favour with Scottish sportsmen cannot be ascertained with any exactness. We know how ardent a votary of Diana and St. Hubert was King James VI., but buck-hunting was his ruling passion in the field. An early notice of fox-hunting as a sport, however, on the part of the upper class, is given in the *Black Book of Taymouth*, occurring in the shape of a letter, dated in 1631, from the Earl of Mar, while residing at Stirling, to Sir Colin Campbell of Glenurchay, whose father had died that same year :—

" To my very loving cousin, the Laird of Glenurchay.

" Loving Cousin,

" Being come in to stay in this town a good part of this winter, I think my greatest sport shall be the hunting of the fox, therefore I will earnestly entreat you to send me with this bearer a couple of good earth dogs. This is my first charge since your father died, and I pray you use me as familiarly as I do you ; for without ceremony, cousin, you shall not have a friend over whom you have greater power than over me. Your loving cousin to do you service.

" MAR.

" Stirling, the 5 of November, 1631.

" What you send me, let it be good, although it should be but one."

Doubtless Sir Colin sent a leash of his best dogs, with which he had scoured the hills and glens of Breadalbane, and the Earl could scarcely fail finding good sport around ·Stirling.

Captain Burt, in his amusing *Letters*, speaks of fox-hunting as he saw it in the Highlands. "There are numbers of foxes," he says; "but they take to the mountains, which are rocky, and sometimes inaccessible to the dogs, of which several have been lost by falling from precipices in the pursuit; for the fox in his flight takes the most dangerous way. But when we happen to kill one of them, it is carried home, through the blessings of the people, like a dangerous captive in a Roman triumph." It was common, indeed, to nail a fox's head to the door of stable or byre, along with a horse-shoe, as a counter-charm against the mischievous pranks of the fairies and the malicious spells of the witches. The Captain writes again that one of the chief complaints of the Highlanders, after being disarmed in 1725, was "that they were de-prived of the means to destroy those noxious animals," foxes and wild-cats, which did them "much more hurt in their poultry, etc., than they yield them profit by their furs; and the eagles do them more mischief than both the others together." * But in this complaint the Highlanders hoaxed the Captain, because in obeying the order for disarmament, they had only given up their worst weapons, the others being carefully concealed for a future rising.

After the middle of last century, when the country had settled down from the disasters of the Rebellion, it came to pass that the people of districts infested with foxes engaged and paid a class of men to root them out. This system prevailed in various parts of Scotland down to the earlier years of the present century. The remuneration of the hunters was sometimes a fixed salary, and sometimes rated at so much per head of the slaughtered foxes, in both cases being provided by a general assessment on the district. When Dr. Johnson was in the Hebrides, in 1773,

---

* *Letters*, Vol. I., p. 138; Vol. II., p. 70.

he found that in the Isle of Skye the head of a fox was worth a guinea to the killer of the animal. The old *Statistical Account of Scotland*, conducted by Sir John Sinclair, gives interesting details of the working of the hired-hunter system at the time the work was issued, namely from 1791 to 1799 : and a few extracts may be made :—

In the united parishes of Lochgoilhead and Kilmorich, Argyleshire, " foxes were formerly very numerous ; but since the land has been chiefly stocked with sheep, the destruction of these animals has become an object of great attention. For this purpose, two, three, or more parishes, according to their extent, join in supporting a fox-hunter, and a pack of dogs. The fox-hunter receives a fixed salary : he is continually perambulating the country, and lives upon his employers ; every tacksman and tenant being obliged to entertain him and his dogs, a specified number of nights in the year, according to the extent of land which he possesses. In consequence of this establishment, a fox is seldom seen."

In the parish of Kirkpatrick-Irongray, Kircudbrightshire, when foxes " begin to kill the sheep anywhere in the parish, the huntsman, who is paid by the country, is sent for, and he seldom fails to unkennel a fox on that hill, or in the woods around it."

In the parish of Lochlee, Forfarshire, poison was used in addition to the operations of the paid huntsman : this being done, " in the winter season, by dragging a piece of salted fish well spiced with powdered *nux vomica*, along a hill side, and leaving it near water. If the fox comes upon the tract, he soon finds the bait, eats it, drinks and expires instantly. The only difficulty lies in finding open water in time of a severe storm, and without this, the *nux vomica* does not kill."

In the parish of Weem, Perthshire, " the foxes, before

the year 1760, made great havoc among the sheep, goats, &c.; but from that time, regular fox-hunters have been employed at fixed salaries, by whose diligence and skill vast numbers of foxes have been destroyed ; so that their number is now greatly reduced."

In Golspie parish, Sutherlandshire, "the fox has still a footing . . . But, much to the honour of this county, upwards of £100 sterling is yearly expended by it for the purpose of extirpating that noxious animal. Every man that chooses may become a fox-hunter : and for every grown fox killed, there is a premium of 5s. out of the sum above specified; for every fox-cub 2s. 6d.; for every female fox having milk in her teats, or being with young, 20s. When a fox-hunter kills a fox, he is obliged to come immediately and present the dead animal to the sight of a Justice of the Peace, or the Minister of the parish ; and to obtain an attestation, in terms of his own declaration, of the parish and the name of the place where he killed the fox, specifying also whether it is male or female, old or young ; and if a female, whether or not it had milk in its teats, or was with young. After this ceremony is over, the huntsman cuts off the ears of the fox, in sight of the inspector, and carries them away carefully, to be kept *in retentis* till the 30th of April, on which day the premium is to be paid. On the 30th of April, unless it falls on a Sunday, the Commissioners of Supply and Justices of the Peace meet in the county burghs, chiefly for the purpose of transacting the fox-business, where all the fox-hunters in the country attend, and produce before the court all the fox-ears they have, with the attestations aforesaid ; and after every examination that may be thought necessary, and their deposition to the truth of the facts contained in their attestations, they receive their money in full. The man that kills the greatest number receives a premium, over and above the modified allowance for each fox."*

Dr. Charles Rogers tells us that, in the times of the hired huntsmen, " several days were occupied annually in the pursuit of the fox, when the entire inhabitants of the district turned out. In Forfarshire these gatherings were convened by the parish beadle while the congregation left church. An ancestor of the writer heard a beadle in Strathmore summon a dispersing congregation to attend at the hunting field, in these words :—

> Ilka man and mither's son,
> Come hunt the tod on Tuesday. †

The section of Somerville's *Chase*, which describes the English fox-hunting, is rivalled in spirit and graphic interest, in a forgotten Scottish poem, *The Grampians Desolate*, by a Perthshire poet, Alexander Campbell, of Tombea, published in quarto, at Edinburgh, in 1804. The author explains that " a mountain fox-hunting differs greatly from the ordinary exertions and pleasures of the chase in situations less elevated, or in an open country where horsemen can follow the pack in the doublings of the game they are in chase of. There are regular fox-hunters in almost every district, that are employed at a yearly allowance, collected as regularly as the minister's stipend." And the hunt among the hills is thus depicted :—

> The hunter to the upland wilds is come,
> A welcome guest !—each *bothan* is his home ;
> His hounds and terriers keen, a yelping train,
> The mountain-echoes now salute again.

---

* Old Statistical Account, Vol. III., p. 176; Vol. IV., p. 532 ; Vol. V., p. 364 ; Vol. XII., p. 134 ; Vol. XXI., p. 220.

† *Scotland, Social and Domestic*, p. 172.

Far out of view, among the airy peaks
The wily prowler into covert sneaks ;
The wary cubs alarm'd, instinctive creep
Hard after, scarcely breathing, silence keep.
  Ere peep of dawn, all ready for the sport,
Forth from the *airidh* to the wilds resort ;
And hunters, hounds, and shepherds' dogs rove wide,
From knoll to knoll, from hill to mountain's side ;
The heath-cock shakes his wing—'tis dawn of day—
Halloo ! the hunt is up—away—away !
He breaks full speed away—swift, swift he flies !
The yell of opening hounds ascends the skies ;
Away, away o'er many a shaggy steep,
Fox, hounds, and huntsmen swift as lightning sweep ;
Beyond the midway far, where cliffs meet sky,
See the sly villain doubling oft on high,—
The pealing pack at fault, impatient, keen,
Range o'er the mountain's brow,—unheard, unseen
The hunters follow, darting swift along,
And fearless bound the craggy wilds among :
From bending heights they far beneath the eye,
Deep in the vale below the thief descry.
Huzza ! again the hounds have gain'd the scent !
Unheeding danger, on their prey intent,
They dash 'midst cliffy windings, shelving rocks,
And rouse the peaceful herds and roving flocks :
The timid mountain-hare, the roe, the hind
Start from their shelter, secret haunts to find.
Ye harmless tenants of these mountains wild,
They thirst not for your blood—ye meek ! ye mild !
Your crafty neighbour of the cavern-rock,
The foe bloodthirsty of the harmless flock,
The canine rangers, full of vengeful fire,
Fain would him worry in instinctive ire.
Lo, now close in upon his utmost speed,
The sanguine pack to mouth him now proceed ;
Without a groan the hardened culprit dies,
The hills resound the hunters' joyous cries !
They pause—and panting dogs stretch'd on the heath
Repose the while, and soon regain their breath ;
And on a dark-brown knoll all now recline,
A homely feast is spread, on which they dine ;

Heart-cheering whisky, oat-cake, goat's milk cheese,
(High cheer that might an ancient hero please !)
Compose the hearty meal—they rest the while ;
Anon to urge anew the pleasing toil,
The huntsman gives the word—and up all spring !
And to their holla mountain-echoes ring—
The game is up again—full speed they fly—
Ere night fall, hunted down, more prowlers die. *

Four years after the issue of Campbell's quarto, an extraordinarily-protracted fox-chase came off in the Highlands. The story goes that on the 8th June, 1808, a fox and a hound, trotting at a slow pace, were observed coming southwards along the highway above Dunkeld, in Perthshire—the fox about fifty yards ahead, but both animals being so fatigued as not to be able to gain upon each other. A countryman on the road easily caught the fox alive, and took both it and the dog to a gentleman's house near by, where poor Reynard drew his last breath through sheer exhaustion. " It was afterwards ascertained," says the narrator, " that the hound belonged to the Duke of Gordon, and that the fox was started on the morning of the King's birthday (4th June), on the top of those hills called *Mona-liadh*, which separates Badenoch from Fort Augustus. From this it appeared that the chase lasted four days, and that the distance travelled, from the place where the fox was unkennelled, to the spot where it was caught, without making any allowance for doubles, crosses, and tergiversations, and as the crow flies, exceeded seventy miles." †

---

* *The Grampians Desolate*, pp. 80, 224. After quoting the above poetical description, we may remark that while England possesses so many popular hunting-songs, the Scottish song books are void of fox-hunting lyrics ; the few songs of that class that exist being of our own day, almost wholly local, and quite unknown to the general public.

† Daniel's *Rural Sports*, Vol. IV., p. 662.

We have now seen the sort of fox-hunting that was so long in vogue in Scotland, and the paucity of early notices of fox-hunting as sport. It was not till about the end of last century that the first pack of hounds was formed for regular sporting purposes, after the English fashion, and this appears to have taken place in the " kingdom of Fife," as shown by Colonel Babington's *Records of the Fife Foxhounds*, published at Edinburgh in 1883. Other counties followed the example. But it cannot be said that fox-hunting was ever a national sport north of the Tweed, notwithstanding the distinguished patronage with which it has been honoured.

CHAPTER V.

THE SALMON RIVER.

And now we'll take the Salmon's story.

The Lentiad.

"THE salmon," says Dame Juliana Berners, "is the most stately fish that any man may angle to in fresh water," and not only the most stately but "a gentle fish," though "cumbrous for to take." Isaak Walton accounts the salmon as "the king of fresh water fish." Hector Boece testifies, for the honour of his country, that "salmon is more plentiful in Scotland than in any other region of the world." And we know that from times, which were regarded as hoary antiquity in the days of Boece, this stately, gentle, and regal fish, so plentiful in the north, had regularly formed a considerable part of the staple Scottish exports. "Centuries before the era of our oldest University," our forefathers carried on trade "with the kindred people of Flanders, Holland, and Normandy; and the hides and wool of our mountains, the salmon of the Dee and Tay, and the herring of our seas, were exchanged against the cloths of Bruges, the wines of Bordeaux and the Rhine, and the table luxuries, as well as the ornaments of dress and art, which found admirers among us long before we appreciated what are now

counted the comforts of life." * The interests of the
salmon fisheries were watched over by the native legislature with fostering and jealous care. Among the earliest
of the Scottish Statutes, dating upwards of six hundred
years back, we meet with laws for the protection and
regulation of this source of national wealth. One of the
Acts promulgated in the reign of Alexander II., ordained
the *Saturday Slap:*

> The water sould be free, that na man sall take fisch in it, fra Saterday
> after the evening song, until Munday, after the sunne rising.

The Salmon fisheries not only furnished a valuable
amount of exports to foreign ports, but also an abundant
portion of the food of the community at home: and
salted salmon and other fish were stored up, along with
the *mart* beef, as winter provisions. When Edward I.
overran Scotland in 1300, "he carried with him his nets
and fishers for the supply of the royal table" from the
Scottish waters: and his son, Edward II., while preparing
to march across the Border, on another invasion, ordered
the citizens of Berwick to provide several hundred barrels
of salmon for the use of his army. The *Liber Albus*, or
White Book of the City of London, compiled in 1419,
mentions the import of Scottish salmon, haddocks, and
herrings. The fishing vocation must have been extensively
pursued on our coasts and rivers ; but an historian has
remarked that "whether it occupied a class of men, who
employed themselves solely in fishing, or was rather
followed but occasionally by persons who applied also to
different labours, cannot be precisely ascertained. Yet is
it probable, that the latter would be the mode in which
the fishing of the Scottish coasts and rivers, was usually

---

* Innes' *Sketches of Early Scotch History*, p. 255.

carried on ; since the sub-division of labour was still very imperfect in Scotland." A great Scottish merchant in the beginning of the fifteenth century, was William Elphin-stone, founder of the commerce of Glasgow, and father of the celebrated Bishop who founded the University of Aberdeen ; and the traffic by which he made his fortune is supposed to have been chiefly the exportation of pickled salmon. In the end of the same century a barrel of Scottish trout or grilse exported to Middleburgh fetched 22s., and a barrel of salmon 25s.*

The use of fixed machinery, such as *Stake Nets*, for the capture of salmon, seems to have been early practised on some parts of the Scottish coasts. The monks of Cupar, in the thirteenth century, had a grant of a *Yair* in the Firth of Tay. But the system was not apparently extended northwards till a later era ; for Boece gives, in an introductory topographical chapter, the following des-cription of what he calls a new mode of fishing on the seaboard of Morayshire :

The people thereof in like sort do use a strange manner of fishing ; for they make a long weele of wicker, narrow-necked, and wide-mouthed, with such cunning, that when the tide cometh the fish shoot themselves into the same, and forthwith are so inclosed that whilst the tide lasteth they cannot go out, nor after the water is gone escape the hands of the fishers.

In 1588, an Account of Scotland—*Discrittione del Regno di Scotia*—was published at Antwerp, by a learned Italian writer, Petruccio Ubaldini, who resided sometime in Scotland as an agent of the English government, in the time of Edward VI. and Queen Elizabeth. He says that

---

* Tytler's *History of Scotland*, (1864) Vol. I., p. 242 ; Heron's *History of Scotland*, Vol. II., p. 277, Vol. III., p. 235 ; Craik's *History of British Com-merce*, Vol. I., p. 192 ; Innes' *Scotland in the Middle Ages*, p. 247 ; *Ledger of Andrew Halyburton.*

he wrote partly from his own personal observation, and partly from that of "trustworthy persons, highly distinguished for their rank, courtesy, and learning." He describes the process of fishing by a stake-net more minutely than Boece, and must either have seen it himself, or received more detailed information than was afforded by that historian. Speaking of the fishermen, he says :—

> Drawing their nets, adapted to this purpose, for a great space through the tideway of the sea, when left dry at low water, and arranging these in a circular form, they fasten them strongly to the ground or sand ; so that, by three or four internal windings, the nets are convoluted, as it were, in the form of a shell ; fastening the said nets accurately in every part, besides the heads, which are again intricately convoluted. When the tide flows, the fish are carried by the current of the water against these nets, and in the mazes of their windings they so entangle themselves by their own efforts, that an escape would be no longer easy, even if the sea should continue at high water for a considerable time ; this, however, having retired, in its ordinary reflux, the nets, with all the fish inclosed in them, are left dry as at first.

The construction of stake-nets still continues very much the same as in the days of Boece and Ubaldini. The system, however, was subsequently abandoned on the east coast during a lengthened period ; for, when it was introduced in the Firth of Tay, in the last quarter of the eighteenth century, and from the mouth of Tay round by Montrose and Aberdeen in 1820, it was regarded as a novelty in these quarters.

The opinion of classic antiquity was not unanimous regarding the use of fish. We read of the fish-ponds and the pisciculture of the Romans, and of the enormous prices paid by their gourmands for rare denizens of the deep. But the Greek author, Dio Chrysostom argues, in an essay on " Kingly Government," that fish is not proper food for personages of high rank ! " Homer," says he, " never introduces " his heroes " as eating fish, though their station was on the banks of a sea, which he uniformly distinguishes by the appellation of the fishy Hellespont ; and this accurate observation was made by Plato. Nor does he regale the suitors themselves on fish, even in the luxurious banquets of these highly delicate and self-indulgent sensualists." As to fishing, Plutarch denounces it "as a filthy, base, illiberal employment, having neither wit nor perspicacity in it, nor worth the labour." The old Celtic tribes of Caledonia, through many generations, were decidedly anti-ichthyophagous in their tastes, despising the piscatory stores of their rivers, lochs, and seas. It is thought that this prejudice arose from the veneration with which they regarded the waters ; and, at all events, fish occur amongst other symbols of Celtic mythology, represented on the sculptured memorial stones scattered up and down the country. Descending to the sixteenth century, we find Cornelius Agrippa, the magician, in his *Vanity of Sciences and Arts*, disparaging fish as "a hard food, not grateful to the stomach, nor yet acceptable in the sacrifices to the gods. Nobody," adds he, with irresistible *naivete*, "nobody ever heard of a fish being immolated !" Speaking of a fish diet and its influence on health, an English writer, of a later age, says that "for the laborious classes it certainly is not adapted to be the sole diet ; but to vegetable food it makes an excellent addition :" and another proposes, as a remedy against dearths, to restore the use of fish to the ancient credit and estimation, holding that "fish is more healthful than flesh, howbeit, that (through the continual use) flesh is more agreeable with our nature." Of course, the idea of fish as "the sole diet" is entirely out of the question. But at present the complaint among the mass of the community is that they cannot, from the general high price, procure such "an excellent addition" as salmon at all : hence the "Bailie Salmon" of *The Lentiad* declares—

> I say, sir, in no place whatever—
> In ocean, lake, or pond, or river,
> Can food be got for human use,
> That goes beyond what I produce.
> There's not a beast in all the land,
> Which reaches any butcher's stand,
> I do not go beyond in price.

It has been further suggested that the frequent or rather the habitual use of salted meat and particularly salted fish may have contributed to the ancient prevalence of leprosy in this and other European countries. The Naturalist of Selborne says—" One cause of this distemper might be, no doubt, the quantity of wretched fresh and salt fish consumed by the commonalty at all seasons, as well as in Lent, which our poor now would hardly be persuaded to touch." The spread of leprosy in Europe, we think, was chiefly attributable to the intercourse with the East opened up by the Crusades, and likewise to the debased sanitary condition of the people. In Scotland this distemper was once a severe scourge, defying the power of medicine. It cut short the days of King Robert Bruce: and so numerous were the infected that public hospitals for their reception were established in the neighbourhood of the more considerable towns. If, however, bad diet had anything to do with the propagation of this fell pest, surely the Scottish Parliament of the year 1400—reign of Robert III.—did a very senseless and reprehensible thing in passing the first clause of the following Act, which appears in the *Regiam Majestatem :*

Chap. 40.   Foule Swyne, or Corrupted Salmon, sould not be sauld.

It is statute, that gif any man bringes to the market corrupt swyne or salmond to be sauld, they sal be taken be the Baillies, and incontinent without any question, sal be send to the lipper folke.

And gif there be na lipper folke, they sall be destroied aluterlie.

On the eve of the outbreak of the Sweating Sickness in

Germany, in 1529, an alarm arose that it was perilous to eat fish. "In the north of Germany, and especially in the March of Brandenburg, eating fish, which were caught in great abundance, was generally esteemed detrimental. Malignant and contagious diseases were said to have been traced to this cause, and it was a matter of surprise that the only food which nature bounteously bestowed was so decidedly injurious. It might be difficult now to discover the cause of this phenomenon, of which we possess only isolated notices, yet, passing over all other conjectures, it is quite credible either that an actual fish poison was developed, or, if this notion be rejected, that a disordered condition of life, such as must be supposed to have existed in a great famine, rendered fish prejudicial to health, in the same way as sometimes occurs after protracted intermittent fevers."* On one occasion, within our own remembrance, popular feeling in London was strongly excited by a like apprehension. This was during the choleraic visitation of 1832. For some months that year salmon were absolutely unsaleable in the London market, to the heavy loss of the tacksmen of Scottish rivers.

It is not to be wondered at that in other times, when salmon, which is now a costly delicacy and obtainable only by the better classes, was so constant an article of diet amongst the common people, they valued it very lightly. Servants and apprentices, wearied of it, as the Israelites of the manna in the wilderness, came at last, it is asserted, to stipulate with their masters, in whose houses they boarded and lodged, that they should not be called upon to partake of salmon oftener than twice or thrice a week. Perhaps their distaste for an unvarying

---

* Professor Hecker's *Epidemics of the Middle Ages*. Third Edition, p. 226.

round of one sort of food was heightened by some such vague dread as that which was slily expressed by the Maybole joiner, John Fletcher, when having been employed at work for a considerable time on a neighbouring farm, he was regaled too frequently on fish. "John," it is said, "had no objections to fish as such, but to partake of them as an important article of diet once or twice a day was rather much for even his patience. He, therefore, rather startled the goodwife one day at dinner by asking, abruptly, 'Are we no telt in the Scripture, mistress, that we'll rise a' flesh?' 'Deed are we, John,' she answered. 'Weel,' rejoined John, 'I dinna see how that can be in our case; I fear we'll rise a' fish.' From that day fish was not so frequently served."† As to apprentices' indentures, the same tradition pervades various countries. But no indenture embodying the specific clause has yet been forthcoming. The late Mr. Ffennel, Commissioner of Fisheries, desirous of testing the assumed fact, publicly offered a reward of £5 for the production of any such document, but the prize was never claimed. In 1870, however, a letter, affording some evidence on the point, appeared in the *North Devon Journal* :—

SIR,—With reference to the controversy in your columns relative to the salmon clause in the indentures of apprentices in former times, allow me to say that I have seen two indentures containing the clause. By one of them the late Mr. John Bowdage, of Axminster, was bound to a baker; by the other, Mr. Emanuel Dommett was bound to Mr. Francis Dight, fellmonger, also of Axminster. The clause restricted the masters to the dining of their apprentices on salmon oftener than twice a week. The price of salmon at that time (the close of the last century) was 2d. to 3d. per lb.—I am, sir, yours truly,

GEO. P. K. PULMAN,
Author of the *Book of the Axe*.

Crewkerne, Dec. 10.

---

† *Reminiscences of Maybole*, p. 12.

In the year 1760, according to the *Newcastle Chronicle* of 1881, salmon was sold in the market of that town at three farthings per pound ; and this was about the period when the apprentices are said to have rebelled against being obliged to take the fish at every meal. Captain Burt, in his *Letters from the North of Scotland*, gives an amusing example of the low estimation in which salmon were held as food by Scottish Highlanders about 1730 :—" The meanest servants, who are not at board wages, will not make a meal upon salmon if they can get anything else to eat. I have been told it here, as a very good jest, that a Highland gentleman, who went to London by sea, soon after his landing passed by a tavern where the larder appeared to the street, and operated so strongly upon his appetite that he went in—that there were among other things a rump of beef and some salmon : of the beef he ordered a steak for himself. ' But,' says he, ' let Duncan have some salmon.' To be short, the cook who attended him humoured the jest, and the master's eating was eightpence, and Duncan's came to almost as many shillings."

At the beginning of the eighteenth century the destruction of spawning or foul salmon during the close season appears to have been very prevalent in Scotland, and unquestionably it was an old and inveterate offence. A broadside, printed at Edinburgh in 1709, contained an anonymous letter to the Earl of Seafield (who had been the last Chancellor of Scotland), on the subject of the salmon fisheries, and showing how great was the annual slaughter of foul fish. " I have known," says the writer, " a fellow not worth a groat kill with a spear in one night's time a hundred black fish or kipper, for the most part full of rawns unspawned :" and he adds—" Even a great many gentlemen, inhabitants by the rivers, are guilty of the same crimes," heedless of "the prodigious treasure thus miserably dilapidated." He reckoned, however, that despite these losses, the Scottish salmon-fishings yielded good results. He had known from 2000 to 3000 barrels, worth about £6 sterling each, exported in one year. "Nay," he continues, "I know Sir James Calder of Muirton alone sold to one English merchant a thousand barrels in one year's fishing. Further, he calculates that if the fisheries were properly protected and cultivated, they should yield 40,000 barrels per annum, valued at £24,000 sterling.* This earnest appeal led to no immediate reformation. No adequate measures were taken for the protection of the fisheries till after more than a hundred years had come and gone.

Was the sport of angling as popular with the ancients as it is with us? Or, can modern times alone claim the merit of having gradually developed a thorough and widely-diffused appreciation of the quiet and yet exhilarating pastime? These questions we will not pretend absolutely to determine. Of course, fishing with hooks, as with cast and drag nets, for obtaining supplies of food, and not for mere recreation, is old enough. The hook, or angle, is mentioned in the Scriptures; and some of the Roman poets make similar references. Thus Ovid, in his *Metamorphoses*—

> With lines and hooks he caught the finny prey ;
> His art was all his livelihood.

But that the Romans, as well as the Egyptians, used hook and line for amusement, is evident from the story of the trick practised by Cleopatra upon Mark Antony, when one of her divers fixed a salted fish to the Triumvir's

---

* Chambers's *Domestic Annals of Scotland*, Vol. III., p. 353.

hook. Still, what, at its best, was the sport on Italian or Egyptian waters—yea, even though Antony had fished for crocodiles on the Nile—as compared with the salmon-angling of our day? The salmon was known to the Romans, but not, it is believed, to the Greeks. We have no means of ascertaining, however, whether the Romans angled for salmon on the rivers in Britain and other provinces where the fish abounded : but we are rather inclined to suspect that all piscatory sport was rather too tame for the generality of a people habituated to sterner pursuits even in their pleasures, and who gloated on the gladiatorial combats and the wild-beast fights in the amphitheatre. Nor did the painted Picts, our forefathers, set much store by the wealth which their waters afforded —the Celtic tribes (as already said) being remarkable for dislike to fish as food.

Of the "monarch of the tide," the royal denizen of Scottish waters, an aquecultural writer has said— "Crowned long ago by acclamation king of fish, learning has done him homage ; the splendour of his destiny has been the theme of modern prophecy; genius has shed her light upon him, and the skill of the engineer has been employed in his service." * Can it, then, be deemed a frivolous task to collect, as we now purpose doing, some *Curiosities of Salmon Fishing ?*—that is to say, to bring under notice some strange and generally romantic modes of capturing salmon, which have been exemplified, at various times, here and there in Scotland.

"There are many linns or pools," says Hector Boece, "which being in some places among the rocks very shallow above and deep beneath, with the fall of the water, and thereto the salmon not able to pierce through

---

* Dr. Peard's *Practical Water-Farming*, p. 51.

the channel, either for swiftness of the course, or depth of the descent, he goeth so near unto the side of the rock or dam as he may, and there adventuring to leap over and up into the linn, if he leap well at first, he obtaineth his desire ; if not, he essayeth eftsoon the second or third time, tilll he return to his countrie. A great fish able to swim against the stream, such as essay often to leap and cannot get over, do bruize themselves and become meazelled ; others that happen to fall upon dry land (a thing often seen), are taken by the people, watching their time, some in cauldrons of hot water, with fire under them, set upon shallow or dry places, in hopes to catch the fattest, by reason of their weight that do leap short."

The River Shin, in Sutherland, emerges from the south-east end of the loch of the same name, and at about a mile's distance from its source, pours its flood over a precipice twenty feet high. We learn from the Statistical Account of Lairg parish, published in 1794, that " the old method of killing the salmon of the Shin (which are, in general, a much larger and coarser fish than any other in Scotland), was by thrusting a long creel or basket, in behind the cascade, at the foot of the rock, and every fish that jumped to get up, was sure to fall in the basket, and kill itself by the fall. When the river happened to be very high a few of the lightest fish would get over the cascade, and make their way to the lake, which was perhaps the circumstance that preserved the breed, the whole run of the water, from the great fall, being so extremely rough and rapid, that there is no sand nor gravel to protect the spawn ; but the fishing company have now erected cruives upon the Shin, near the place where it discharges itself into the Kyle of Sutherland.*

---

* Sinclair's *Statistical Account of Scotland*, Vol. XI., p. 570.

Another remarkable fall is the *Red Linn*, on the River Beauly, at Kilmorack, in Inverness-shire. The stream, plunging down a dozen of feet, collects in a pool, surrounded with rocks, which are only a little higher than the surface of the water. When the salmon, in trying to clear the cascade, fail in their spring, they fall back sometimes on the craggy banks. In other days, the country people were in the habit of laying down turf and branches of trees along the edge of the rocks, so as to form a parapet, whereby a fish falling within it was prevented from wriggling back into the water; and we are assured by the old statistical writers, that in this way, eight, twelve, and twenty salmon were frequently secured in a single night. But a far more ingenious plan was hit upon by one of the Lords of Lovat, the masters of the river, enabling him to make an apparently incredible boast. He "caused a small boiler full of water to be placed over a fire on this rock," and, according to the tradition of the district, "some of the fish, being driven back by the current, fell often into the said boiler. A fish caught and boiled in this manner was sometimes served up to dinner; so that his lordship often surprised strangers by telling them that the fish now before them had leaped out of the Beauly into the very pot in which it was boiled; and bringing them sometimes to the spot, what he gave out was confirmed by ocular demonstration." Our informant further states that on this pool he had "seen some of the neighbouring inhabitants fish, by standing on the rock above it with a long pole. On one end of this pole are fixed three large hooks joined together, and turned back to back. The person who fishes with the pole dips it in the pool, and after waiting for about half-a-minute, draws it up with a jerk, and generally hooks a fish by some part of his body."* Moreover, the famous Simon of Lovat, who lost his head on Tower-hill, in 1746, carried on a profitable export of Beauly salmon, the capture of which " was generally accomplished by men watching on the rocks, and spearing them as they attempted to leap the waterfall—a perilous occupation, since it added the shock and struggle with a nimble and strong animal to the natural hazard of clambering among precipices."†

At the Linn of Avon, among the wilds of Banffshire, it was once the custom to hang a capacious bag-net from a strong crossbeam right across the cataract, so that the salmon, if they leaped short, fell into this receptacle, and were taken. A certain worthy of the locality, with confused notions of *meum et tuam* in his head, and who was unconnected with this fishing, though he had a penchant for salmon, occasionally stole to the Linn under cloud of night, when he knew that nobody would be there, and quietly drawing the bag-net to land, appropriated its contents, after which he carefully replaced it in its proper position, and slipped off unseen with his plunder. He continued this nefarious game for a considerable time, with varying success, and without incurring the slightest suspicion. At length, grown careless and foolhardy in his darkling work at the fall, he one night lost his footing on the wet crags, and tumbled down headlong—not into the raging torrent, but, fortunately, into the bag. Never before had such a catch been made, and there he swung, like Mahomet in his coffin, suspended helplessly betwixt earth and heaven, and drenched with the foam and spray of the linn. Had not the beam and tackle been stout, his adventure would have ended in the boiling depths

---

* Sinclair's *Statistical Account*, Vol. XIII., p. 512; Vol. XX., p. 403.
† Burton's *Lives of Lord Lovat and Duncan Forbes*, p. 142.

below. He had no means of extrication from a predicament so ludicrous and withal so full of peril. For hours, which seemed ages, he lay huddled in the net, shivering to the core with wet, cold, affright, and the terror of inevitable discovery. Morning dawned, and soon the owner of the bag-net came to the spot. Rubbing his eyes again and again to make sure that he saw clearly, so astounded was he by the sight of so exceeding queer a fish caught in the toils. The trembling culprit confessed everything, and was relieved with a suitable admonition. Thenceforth, as we may be sure, he scrupulously avoided going near the linn either by night or by day.*

In the middle of the fourteenth century the shire of Caithness owned the sway of a powerful baron, named Roland Cheyne—perhaps an ancestor of the brave young squire of the same name whose chivalry at Harlaw was chaunted by old Elspeth Mucklebackit. The baron's castle of Dirlet stood on a rocky height bordering a deep pool of the Thurso river. In that pool, immediately under the walls, he erected a salmon cruive, which was so cunningly constructed that the entrance of a fish within it rang a warning-bell !† A like story is told of Lochmore Castle, on the banks of the lake of that name, about eight miles from Dirlet. There, it is said, the capture of a salmon was announced to the whole family by the ringing of a bell, which hung in a room of the castle, and was connected by a cord with the machine in the stream below.‡

One of the most picturesque of the tributaries of the Tay is the Tummel, which, after joining with the Garry,

---

* Glenmore's *Highland Legends*, p. 85.
† Mackay's *History of the House and Clan of Mackay*, p. 42.
‡ Sinclair's *Statistical Account*, Vol. XIX., p. 54.

flows into the former river about half-a-mile below the thriving village of Logierait. Before uniting with the Garry near Faskally, the Tummel is a rapid and impetuous Highland torrent, forming many small cascades in its troubled course, and also a great cataract, known as "The Falls of Tummel," *par excellence*, at a short distance above Faskally, where the rushing current precipitates itself over a mass of rock from sixteen to eighteen feet high, constituting one of the finest falls in Scotland. The rock, however, prevents the salmon ascending the river for the purpose of spawning, and but for this barrier they would have a free run of some five-and-twenty miles to Loch Rannoch, through what would prove the best spawning ground in the district. The fish, in attempting to leap the falls, have been often caught by baskets and otherwise, as was the case when Mr. Pennant visited the scene during his Scottish Tour of 1772. "Salmons," he says, "annually force their passage even up this furious cataract ; and are taken here in a most artless manner : a hamper, fastened to a wicker-rope, pinned into the cleft of the rock by a stick, is flung into the stream : now and then a fish, in the fall from its effort to get up, drops into this little ware. It is not to be supposed that the owner can enrich himself by the capture : in fact, the chance of his good fortune is hired out at the annual rent of one pound fourteen shillings. At other times, the fisher flings into the stream below a crowfoot, or caltrop, fastened to a long rope. On this instrument, the salmons often transfix themselves, and are drawn up to land. Another method, of much risk to the adventurer, is at times practised. A person seats himself on the brink of the precipice, above the cataracts, and fixes one foot in the noose of a wicker-cord : here he expects the leap of a salmon : armed with a spear, the moment the fish rises, he darts his weapon at the hazard of falling into the water by his own effort, or the struggles of his prey."*

"Down by the Tummel" we have thus gleaned some Curiosities of Salmon Fishing; but our quest fails to discover such on the "banks of the Garry." Still, we cannot quit that romantic Highland river without some pleasant reminiscence congenial to our theme, and therefore we quote the following feminine effusion, from Mr. Pennant's book, commemorating the appearance of two fair and titled dames as anglers on Garry's banks :—

ON THE DUCHESS OF ATHOLL AND LADY WRIGHT FISHING AT ATHOLL HOUSE.

BY A LADY.

Where silver-footed Garry nimbly flows,
  Whose verdant banks the nymphs and naiads love,
Where nature ev'ry blooming sweet bestows,
  Not less delightful than Idalia's grove ;

As contemplation led my wand'ring feet
  Along the margin of the crystal flood,
The feather'd songsters hail'd the sweet retreat,
  And gentle zephyrs whisper'd thro' the wood.

Charm'd with the scene, silent a while I gaz'd,
  Intently list'ning to the murm'ring stream,
In grateful transports nature's God I prais'd,
  And long my soul pursu'd the rapt'rous theme.

At length I heard, or fancy form'd the tale,
  A gentle voice in mournful notes complain ;
Soft echo bore the accents thro' the vale,
  And thus the mourner seem'd to breathe his pain :

" Why did I idly leave the coral groves,
  Where safety on the breast of silence lies ?
Danger still waits the heedless fool that roves,
  And in pursuit of fleeting bliss he dies.

---

* *A Tour in Scotland : 1772.* Part II., p. 56.

" One fatal day, as near the brink I stray'd,
　　Two pleasing forms lean'd o'er the trembling brook,
　Their gentle smiles an artless mind betray'd ;
　　Mischief sure never wore so fair a look.

" Each held a magic wand with wondrous grace,
　　A pendant line convey'd the tempting bait ;
　O sight, portentous to the finny race,
　　Fraught with the dire command of cruel fate !

" My tender mate play'd fearless by my side ;
　　With eager joy she snatch'd the hidden dart,
　Instant, alas ! I lost my lovely bride ;
　　What racking torture seiz'd my wounded heart.

" E'er since that hour, to pining grief a prey,
　　My flowing tears increase my native flood,
　In melancholy sighs I waste the day,
　　And shun the commerce of the scaly brood.

" Shou'd chance this mournful tale at Blair relate,
　　Where dwell the dang'rous fair who caus'd my pain,
　They who can love so well, wou'd mourn my fate,
　　And ne'er disturb our harmless race again." *

This elegiac strain on the death of a trout is quite in keeping with the sentimentality of our eighteenth century pastoral poetry. It reminds us of the occasion when Goldsmith, holding forth, in Johnson's presence, about making animals in fable talk in character, referred to little fishes, adding that " the skill consisted in making them talk like little fishes." Johnson could not forbear laughing at the idea, upon which Goldy observed—" Why, Dr. Johnson, this is not so easy as you seem to think ; for if you were to make little fishes talk, they would talk like *whales*." Our readers can judge for themselves whether the lament of the Garry trout fulfils the Goldsmithian requirement.

---

* *A Tour in Scotland :* Part II., p. 450.

Another Perthshire stream, the Ericht, supplies us with curiosities. The Ericht springs from the Grampian hills, but along that part of its course which runs through Glenshee, a pass leading into Aberdeenshire, it is called the Shee ; then it changes its name to the Blackwater ; and the Blackwater being afterwards joined by the Ardle, also from a Grampian source, the confluent waters receive the name of Ericht. The river flows through the beautiful vale of Glenericht, and falls into the Isla, about two miles north of Coupar-Angus. In some parts the banks of the Ericht are low, and therefore liable to be overflowed in times of spate, but in other places they " ascend like lofty wa's," towering in rugged grandeur. What lover of the picturesque who has visited Craighall can ever forget the romantic scene ? North of Blairgowrie, the river, for the space of a couple of miles, rushes through a ravine, the rocky sides of which rise frequently to a height of 300 feet.

A statistical writer of 1792 stated that "sportsmen look upon the water of Ericht as one of the finest rivers for rod-fishing, both for trout and salmon." At that time the principal fishing on the Ericht was at the Keith, near Rattray, where the river rolls down over a ledge of rock, the basin beneath being a great resort of salmon preparing to try their agility against the obstruction ; and the mode of capturing them had been peculiar to the place beyond the memory of man. If the river was in flood, a bag-net, attached to a long hazel handle, perfectly elastic, was let down by fishermen perched on the brink of the overhanging cliffs ; but when the stream was low and clear, the fishermen plied their craft only after sunset, when they threw a thin clay, resembling wrought mortar, into the pool to darken the water, and then let down the bag-net. A later writer, in 1843, described this *modus*

operandi as then in vogue, with an important addition :
" There is still another expedient put in practice for the
destruction of the fish. When the river is small, its
breadth from rock to rock, about thirty yards below the
fall, is not more than from six to eight feet ; and at this
narrow a net nearly of the same form as those already
described, but shorter in the handle, and sufficiently large
to fill up nearly the whole space from side to side, is put
down into the water, as near to the bottom as possible,
and the fish are dislodged from under the rocks above,
and forced downwards by means of a long pole with a
mass of red cloth at the end of it, which is pushed under
the rocks. Terrified and confused by the noise and
splashing, and the glare of the uncouth instrument with
which it is performed, the salmon rush blindly down to
escape it, and fall into the net placed to intercept them.
Frequently, however, they escape the danger, either by
getting past or under the net, or by darting out of it again
before it can be raised to the surface.* But the days of
salmon-fishing on the Ericht are over. How different was
it when, in 1804, a pool, called the *Coble-Pool*, yielded 336
salmon and grilse at a single haul !

The *blazing* or *burning* of rivers which long prevailed
over Scotland, but is now almost extinct, claims a passing
notice in the present connection. A vivid description of
the custom as it was practised, on the Borders last
century, occurs in *Guy Mannering*. A tribe of Highlanders inhabiting Strathavon, Banffshire, had a habit of
taking their fish-spears with them when they went to the
kirk of a Sunday, that they might strike salmon on their
way, which led along the banks of the river Avon. When
they reached the place of worship, they set their spears

---

* *New Statistical Account of Perthshire* : Blairgowrie, p. 920.

against the gable, and devoutly heard service, but when it was over they resumed their weapons, and beguiled their homeward route with fresh sport.*

Salmon - poachers generally employed the *leister* and the *torch* during the close-time, the very time when the fish were unfit as food, and needed protection most for the welfare of the fisheries ; but until the year 1828 there was no adequate protection to our salmon waters—not for want of legislative enactments, but because their enforcement, formerly a matter of difficulty, had latterly become useless for the object in view.   The Act of 1828 declared *blazing* unlawful, prohibiting, under a penalty, any person using " any light or fire of any kind, in or for the taking or with intent to take any salmon, grilse, sea-trout, or other fish of the salmon kind :" and it also established a protective force for the rivers.   Severe was the struggle which ensued with the *blazing* poachers. In Perthshire—especially in the eastern district—bands assembling in disguise, with blackened faces, like companies of Guizards, defied the law with a courage and persistency worthy of a better cause.   Night after night the Isla was blazed by these resolute bands, between whom and the watchers many a tough "skrimmage" was waged in the darkness.   But the power of law gradually got the upper hand.   On the Earn, too, and in other quarters, similar contests took place with the like result. In 1836, a witness examined before a Committee of the House of Commons on the Scottish Salmon Fisheries, gave evidence as to the practice of *blazing*—which by that time had much diminished—on the Teith.   The poachers, he said " use what they call a blaze and a spear ; there is generally one person walks in the centre, having a faggot,

---

* Glenmore's *Highland Legends*, p. 92.

made of dry fir, sometimes dry broom, put on a pole; this he carries up high above his head, and there is generally a person walking on each side of him with a spear each, what we call a lister, with three prongs ; the effect of the light is to show clearly the fishes in the stream." But now, happily for the peace and morality of the country districts, the leister and the blaze are seldom seen in any part of Scotland.

Another fashion was peculiar to the Solway Firth, where, during the ebb of the tide, the salmon left in the pools on the sands were dextrously speared by horsemen. This sport has been depicted in *Redgauntlet.*

The banks of our salmon rivers have often echoed the confused clamour of a sport, with which, in its hurrying bustle and excitement, the Waltonian art, the "contemplative man's recreation," bears no comparison. The otter, that

> Water-wolf, of species undefined,
> Or fish, or quadruped, or both conjoined,

was formerly a constant object of pursuit on Scottish streams, and the otter-hunt ranked high in the category of national diversions,—the animal being classed, by the old writers on hunting, with the badger and the wild-cat, as affording "greate dysporte," though conventionally belonging to the "rascal" kind.   But this water-wolf has now disappeared from most of its long-accustomed haunts, and its chase, north of the Tweed, has almost become a thing of the past.   Peculiarly obnoxious to the piscatorial interests of the rivers, the otter is held in detestation by the angler.   "I am, sir, a brother of the angle, and therefore an enemy to the otter," quoth old Isaak ; "for you are to note that we anglers all love one another, and therefore do I hate the otter, both for my own and for their sakes who are of my brotherhood." On the other hand, the "base vermin" has been regarded with far different feelings by the peasantry of a water-side. The Highland people affectionately call it *caraid nam bochd*, "the poor man's friend," because of its habit of eating no more than a bit from the back or shoulder of a salmon, and then leaving the fish lying on the bank, to be picked up by the first passer-by. In Scotland it has been an old belief that the otters have a king, of larger size than the rest of the species, and farther distinguished by having his coat streaked or varied with white. His skin, moreover, was thought to possess inestimable virtues to mankind. It was an antidote for infectious diseases: the Highlanders were anxious to line their targets with it to ensure victory in battle; and mariners valued it as an infallible preservation against shipwreck at sea. But, as we are told, "the otter-king is very rarely seen, and very hard to be killed;" and he is never killed without the sudden death of a man or an animal at the same moment!

The otter is capable of being utilised in the capture of salmon. An English gentleman had one, who followed him with his dogs when he went to hunt other otters; but though the hounds did not molest their queer companion, they would hunt no otters in his presence, upon which account, although he was useful in fishing, and in driving the trouts towards the net, his owner had to part with him. A man near Inverness had likewise a tame otter, which was frequently employed in fishing, and would take eight or ten salmon in a day. When one was taken from it, it dived for another, and when tired and satisfied with eating its share, it curled itself round and fell asleep, in which state it was generally carried home. An otter in the possession of a gentleman farmer near Coupar-Angus was quite domesticated. It

was as tame as a dog, and slept every night with one of
its master's sons. In the day time it regularly frequented
a loch in the neighbourhood for the purpose of procuring
fish, but would always come out of the water when called
by any person of the family. In 1807, a young man, at
Lochside, in the parish of Blairgowrie, having shot at and
wounded a young otter, carried it home, where it speedily
recovered, and became as tame as a lap-dog. It accompanied its master to the lochs and rivers in the vicinity,
where it dived for fish, brought them to land, and
returned for more.* Recently, a correspondent of a
London sporting paper suggested that the otter might be
employed in catching trout on lochs where boats are
scarce or difficult to procure ; but, in our opinion, there is
little chance of the animal coming into favour, under any
circumstances, as a substitute for the rod or the net.

Cormorants, too, were trained to fish for the amusement
of their masters ; and it appears that this fashion, which had
been long practised by the Chinese, was introduced into
Europe during the sixteenth century. Our British Solomon,
James I., kept cormorants and otters on the ponds in
the London parks. This is shown by the Pell Records.
In France, Henry IV., Louis XIII., and the *Grande
Monarque* patronised cormorant fishing on the ponds
and canals of Fontainebleau, where there was a " Keeper."

But the sport is not extinct in England. The
Field of 18th October, 1890, contains a communication
from Mr. F. H. Salvin of Cambridgeshire, in which he
states that he " was the first who revived cormorant fishing in England many years ago," and he gives " some of
his experiences of the training and management of these
birds, both at home and in the field."

---

* Daniel's *Rural Sports*, Vol. I., pp. 519, 520 ; Vol. IV., p. 55.

Fishing with geese was a sport often enjoyed in bye-gone days on the waters of the beautiful Lake of Menteith, in south-western Perthshire. " A line with a baited hook was fastened to the leg of a goose, which was then placed on the water of the lake. A boat containing a party of lords and ladies followed the bird. Soon a marauding pike took hold of the bird. A capture ensued. The splashing, floundering, wheeling of the combatants was overpowering as a source of merriment, till at length amidst the clapping of hands and waving of handker-chiefs, the goose proved triumphant, and bore a prisoner to land, his sharp-toothed adversary." *

* Dr. Rogers' *Scotland, Social and Domestic*, p. 152.

CHAPTER VI.

THE RACE COURSE.

See, the course throng'd with gazers, the sports are begun,
The confusion but hear !—I'll bet you, sir,—Done, done !
Ten thousand strange murmurs resound far and near,
Lords, hawkers, and jockeys assail the tired ear :
While with neck like a rainbow, erecting his crest,
Pamper'd, prancing, and pleas'd, his head touching his breast,
Scarcely snuffing the air, he's so proud and elate,
The high-mettled racer first starts for the plate.

Charles Dibdin.

HORSE-RACING is a sport of high antiquity. Great was its repute among the ancient Greeks and Romans. When all that was glorious in the arts of war and peace dignified the Grecian States, the most exciting and admired features of the Olympic Games were the horse-races and chariot-races ; and famous monarchs themselves did not disdain to lay aside their pomp, and become competitors in those contests. King Hiero of Syracuse, the munificent patron of Æschylus and Pindar and other poets, rode his own horse, Phrenicus, and won the Olympic crown ; and King Philip of Macedon entered the course mounted on the brother to Bucephalus. Pindar composed his first Olympic ode in celebration of Hiero's triumph. Sophocles, in his tragedy of *Electra*, has left a graphic

picture of the chariot-races, which Pindar also commemorates in glowing verse ; and Ovid addresses one of his
Love Elegies " to his Mistress at the Horse Race ":—

> " Not in the Circus do I sit to view
> The running horses, but to gaze on you ;
> Near you I choose an advantageous place,
> And whilst your eyes are fix'd upon the race,
> Mine are on you."

Leaving the Olympic and the Roman races, and
descending the stream of time, we find that in mediæval
England both Saxon and Norman amused themselves
with the running of fleet steeds. Races were held in
Smithfield as early as the reign of Henry II. The
seasons for the sport were usually Easter and Whitsun-
tide, which, however, were latterly changed from religious
motives. The prizes were silver bells. Several running-
horses were purchased for Edward III., at the price of 20
marks, or £13 6s. 8d. each, and others at 25 marks.
Down to the seventeenth century, horse-racing in England,
as Strutt informs us, " was considered as a liberal pastime,
practised for pleasure rather than profit, without the least
idea of reducing it to a system of gambling"; but it soon
afterwards degenerated, for Burton, in his *Anatomy of
Melancholy*, speaking of the recreations of country-folks,
and characterizing horse-races as amongst " the disports
of greater men, and good in themselves," satirically adds,
" though many gentlemen by that means gallop quite out
of their fortunes." The modern system of horse-racing
may be said to date from the reign of James I. Public
race meetings were then first instituted ; and the prizes
were still bells—gold and silver. It was long said that in
a moment of extravagance, when his purse was better
lined than ordinary, the British Solomon, who was a most
ungainly rider, threw away £500 sterling money for an

Arabian, which proved a failure, being soundly beaten by English horses, but we find from Rice's *History of the British Turf* that the price was only £154 sterling. The short-lived Prince Henry was a zealous supporter of racing; and the unfortunate King Charles, before he found more serious matters to absorb his attention, was fond of the sport,—but in his time some English writers were of opinion that stout horses were decreasing in the kingdom, owing " to the strong addiction of the country to hunters and running horses which were bred only for speed." Curious to relate, the Protector, Oliver Cromwell, Puritan as he was, kept at least a couple of racers, the *White Turk* and the *Coffin Mare !*—though, when in dread of Royalist conspiracy, he dared " suffer no assemblies, not so much as horse-races," as is charged against him in Colonel Titus' extraordinary tract, *Killing no Murder*, which is said to have hastened the "tyrant's" death. The Restoration revived all "the old familiar" English sports and pastimes, against which the sour spirits of the Commonwealth, misunderstanding national character, habits, predilections, had zealously set their faces, backed by the pains and penalties of law. The Merry Monarch gave the turf every encouragement; established meetings at Datchet Mead, and also at Newmarket; entered horses in his own royal name; and bought mares from Barbary and other countries for the improvement of the English breed. Race prizes now rose in value to a hundred guineas each, and it was the custom to engrave the names and pedigree of the winning horses upon these trophies of victory. William of Orange and Mary his Queen patronised the turf liberally, adding several plates to those which Royalty had usually bestowed. More new plates were given by Queen Anne, whose husband, Prince George of Denmark, owned a number of capital racers. Silver plates as prizes were abolished by George I., who gave instead a hundred guineas, to be paid in specie. Let us notice, however, that in 1725, a diverting race was advertised to be run at Ripon, in Yorkshire, namely—" *The Lady's Plate* of £15 value, by any horse that was no more than five years old the last grass. *Women* to be the riders : each to pay one guinea entrance : three heats, and twice round the common for a heat."

Probably the Scots practised the amusement of competing with fleet horses at as early a period as their neighbours south of the Tweed, though, in process of time, the English became the chief promoters of the sport. Or, it might be conjectured that as Horse-racing was common among the Normans and Saxons, the influx of both into Scotland, after the Conquest, may have introduced this pastime to the northern people. But without wandering in the antiquity of that era, we shall farther descend to the sixteenth century, when public horse-racing took place statedly at several towns in Scotland. Respecting the conditions of the sport we have no information, nor do we know anything about the breed and training of the horses. All that we are able to do is to gather together a variety of scattered notices showing that horse-racing existed in Scotland at the period mentioned.

The earliest notices of the sport occur in 1504, during the reign of James IV. On the 15th April that year, the Lord High Treasurer of Scotland enters in his Accounts a payment " to Thomas Boswell, he laid down in Leith to the wife of the King's Innis, and to the boy that ran the King's horse, 18s. : " and on 2d May following there is a payment of 28s. " to Dande Doule whilk he wan frae the King on horse-racing." Our next authority is Sir David Lindsay of the Mount, Lord Lyon King at Arms

under James V. In Sir David's poem, the *Complaint*,
where he enumerates the different games and pastimes
which the King enjoyed in his boyhood, horse-races are
ncluded :—

> Some gart him raiffell at the racket,
> Some harled him to the hurly-hacket ;
> And some to show their courtly corsis (persons)
> Wad ride to Leith, and rin their horses,
> And wichtly wallop over the sands :
> Yea neither spared spurs nor wands ;
> Casting galmounds, with bends and becks,
> For wantonness, some brak their necks.

The sands of Leith continued to be used as a Race-
ground till the year 1816, when the annual meeting was
transferred to Musselburgh. The neighbouring town of
Haddington had a Horse-race in 1552, the prize being a
silver bell. Under date of 10th May, the records of the
burgh contain an entry to this effect: "The whilk day,
John Forrois, burgess of Haddington, came cautioner that
ane worthy and mighty Lord, George Lord Seytoun, shall
bring the Silver Bell that his horse won upon the 10th day
of May, the year of God I^m V^c Fifty twa years, to the
said burgh of Haddington upon the third day of November
the same year of God, and present the same to the
Provost and Bailies of the said burgh of Haddington,
with an augmentation like as the said Lord pleases to
augment for his honour, and the same Bell to be run for
the said day, sa the winner thereof may have the same
again ; and for observing of thir premises the said John
Forrois has acted (bound) himself in the common burgh
of Haddington, the said X day of May, the year of God
above specified." From this it would seem that the race
for the bell was held half-yearly.

Towards the end of 1575, the Regent Morton visited
the Border for the purpose of holding Courts of Justice ;

and while he was at Dumfries, "there entered many gentlemen of England," says the contemporary author of the *Historie and Life of King James the Sext*, "for to behold the Regent's Court, where there was great provocation made for riding of horses; and by fortune, my Lord Hamilton had there a horse so well bridled, and so speedy, that although he was of a meaner stature from other horses that essayed their speed, he overcame them all a great way upon Solway sands, whereby he obtained great praise both of England and Scotland that time."

It is said that the defeat of the Spanish Armada, in 1588, had some influence in promoting the taste for Horse-racing in Scotland, from the fact that one or two of the ships being wrecked on the west coast, a number of fine Spanish horses got ashore, and proved remarkable for their swiftness. But the tradition seems to rest on no tangible foundation.

An old annual festival held at the town of Peebles, on *Beltane*, or the second of May, was distinguished by horse-races; but such gatherings on the Border was frequently attended with broils and bloodshed. In 1608, therefore, the Peebles race was prohibited, as a nuisance, by the Scottish Government. The Lords of Secret Council issued an order, on 28th April, to the effect that being "informed that there is ane Horse-race appointed to be at Peebles the——day of May next to come, whereunto great numbers of people of all qualities and ranks, intends to repair, betwixt whom there being quarrels, private grudges, and miscontentment, it is to be feared that at their meeting upon fields, some troubles and inconvenients shall fall out amangs them, to the break of His Majesty's peace and disquieting of the country, without (unless) remeed be provided; therefore the Lords of Secret Council has discharged, and by the tenor hereof discharges, the said Horse-race, and ordains that the same shall be nowise holden nor kept this year ; for which purpose ordains letters to be direct, to command, charge, and inhibit all and sundry His Majesty's lieges and subjects by open proclamation at the Market-cross of Peebles and other places needful, that none of them presume nor take upon them to convene and assemble themselves to the said race this present year, but to suffer that meeting and action to depart and cease, as they and ilk ane of them will answer upon the contrary at their highest peril." We shall return to Peebles at a later stage.

The royal burgh of Stirling had its annual Horse-race in the end of the sixteenth century, if not earlier—an entry in the Town Council books, of date 18th April, 1598, being to the following effect: " Ane bell of fine silver, weighing twa ounce and ane half, to be provided eight days before Pasch (Easter), and delivered to the Magistrates on Pasch Tuesday," as the prize for a Horse-race."

Paisley, too, bestirred itself in patronage of the Turf. The Council minutes of April, 1608, contains an order " that a silver bell be made of four ounce weight, with all diligence, for a Horse-race yearly to be appointed within this burgh, and the bounds and day for running thereof to be set down by my Lord Abercorn, Lord Paisley, and Kilpatrick." At Paisley, in May, 1620, there were two prizes given for the principal race : 1st. the silver bell, " with the Burgess arms thereupon, for that year, together with the rest of the gold that shall be given in with the said bell ;" and 2nd, a double angel ; while another prize for " an after-shot race," was " a furnished saddle." The Paisley bell is still preserved, and is considered as old as that of Lanark. Generally the prize-bells of the time weighed about 4oz., and remained as the property of the towns which offered them—the winners being allowed to retain them for a year respectively.

Racing appears to have been in great vogue at Cupar Fife and Dunfermline about the beginning of the seventeenth century. A curious Act of Caution, dated 4th April, 1610, concerning the Races at the latter town, is copied in the burgh books, and quoted in Seton's *Memoir of Alexander Seton, Earl of Dunfermline*:—

Cautionry for production of the Race Bell upon the fourth day of April, 1611.

At Dunfermling 19 day of April, ano 1610, in presence of John Anderson and James Mochrie, Bailies of the burgh.

The whilk day, in presence of the saids Bailies, compeared personally Mr. James Douglas, the Schoolmaster, burgess of the said burgh, and upon his awin proper confession, acted him, his heirs, executors, and assigns, as cautioner and surety for David Boswell, brother german to Sir John Boswell, of Balmuto, knight : That the said David, or others in his name, shall exhibit and produce, before the Provost and Bailies of the said burgh, in the Tolbooth thereof, upon the fourth day of April, in the year of God sixteen hundred and eleven years next to come, at ten hours before noon, the silver Race bell double overgilt, his Majesty's name and arms graven thereupon, weighing   pertaining to ane noble lord, Alexander Earl of Dunfermline, Lord Fyvie and Urquhat, High Chancellor of Scotland, Bailie heritable principal of the regality of Dunfermline, delivered this day to the said David, in custody and keeping, by command and ordinate of the said noble Earl, by reason of the said David's black horse winning the custody and keeping thereof by running frae Conscience Brig to the Brig of Urquhat in company with other twa horses, viz., ane dapple grey horse belonging to Sir William Monteth of Kers, knight, and the other ane brown horse belonging to Lewis Monteth, his brother german, and won frae them the race. And that the said David Boswell shall deliver and produce the said bell in the like and also good state as he now receives the same, under the pains of five hundred merks money Scots, to be paid by the said Cautioner to the said noble Earl in case of failure, and the said David Boswell compearing personally, demitting his awin jurisdiction, and duly submitting him in this case to the jurisdiction of the Provost and Bailies of the said burgh, of his awin confession, acted him to free and relieve the said Mr. James Douglas, his Cautioner, of this present Cautionry between him and the said Bailies, and of other penalties. The said Bailies interponed their authority thereto, and ordains execution of poinding and warding to pass hereupon in case of failure of production of the bell at the day and in manner above specified.

4th April, 1611.

This act delete be reason David Boswell produced the horse race bell, induciæ this day.

JOHN ANDERSON, Bailie.

In 1621, the Lords Morton, Boyd, and Abercorn, entered into an Indenture at Hamilton regarding a proposed race : the agreement providing that the course was to be " three mett miles of Cupar race in Fife," the stakes ten double angels for each horse, the winner receiving the whole ; and each rider " eight Scots stane weight."

But by this time betting on races seems to have risen to such a height that the Parliament of Scotland, in August, 1621, passed an Act declaring that all money won at cards and dice, or in wagers at horse-races, above 100 merks Scots, should belong to the poor of the parish in which it was won :—

If it shall happen any man to win any sums of money at Carding or Dicing, attour (above) the sum of an hundred merks, within the space of twenty-four hours ; or to gain at wagers upon Horse races, any sum attour the said sum of an hundred merks ; the surplus shall be consigned, within twenty-four hours thereafter, in the hands of the Treasurer of the Kirk, if it be in Edinburgh, or in the hands of such of the Kirk-Session, in country parochines, as collects and distributes money for the poor at the same, to be employed always upon the poor of the parish where such winning shall happen to fall out. And to the effect that either excess in play may be thus restrained, or, at the least, excessive winning may be employed as said is, our Sovoreign Lord, by Act of his supreme Court of Parliament, gives full power and commission to the Bailies and Magistrates of Burghs, the Sheriffs and Justices of Peace in the country, to pursue and convene all such persons, for all winning at Cards, Dice, and Horse-races, which shall happen to be made by any person, by and attour (over and above) the said sum of an hundred merks money aforesaid: and in case the Magistrate informed thereof refuse to pursue for the same, the party informer shall have action against the said Magistrate for double the like sum, the one half whereof to be given to the poor, and the other half to the party informer,

We shall come to an instance in which this statute was made operative at the distance of a century and a half after its enactment.

The first notice of Horse-races at Perth, where the North and South Inches afforded the requisite facilities for the sport, occurs in the Town Council records for 1613. That year, a prize, consisting of a silver bell, presented by Ninian Graham, laird of Garvock, in name of John Graham, laird of Bogside, was run for and won. The course was then, and for a considerable while afterwards, on the South Inch. On the 6th of May, 1615, the Council ordered six stakes to be placed there "for the riding of the horse-race in time coming." Not long after this period, a change in race-prizes began to take place gradually over the country—cups, bowls, or other pieces of plate, being substituted for the bells. Under date of 14th May, 1625, the Town Council of Glasgow "ordains the Horse Race to be proclaimed to the 25th day of May instant, and the Cup to be made." On 14th February, 1631, the Perth Town Council resolved to convert three silver bells, weighing in all eleven ounces, into a prize Cup, to be run for after Palm Sunday. Next month, 21st March, the minutes speak of the new prize cup, weighing 8 oz., obtained in lieu of the three silver bells, as these had been found "unsuitable." The race was held on the day after Palm Sunday: posts were erected on the South Inch: and the cup was won by Thomas Tyrie of Drumkilbo, with his horse called *Kildair*.

The silver race-bell which the burgh of Lanark possessed at the period under notice is still extant, and has been frequently competed for on the course in our own times. According to the Lanark tradition, it was presented to the burgh in 1160 by King William the Lion, but the story is palpably absurd. The bell does not seem older than the early part of the seventeenth century. It is of the usual form, four inches high under the ring handle, and four inches across the circular mouth, which is closed with a dome-shaped silver plate, having a cross-shaped opening in the centre, terminating in quatrefoils. It bears engraved on the front the Lanark arms, and also the monogram, " R. D.," which probably denotes that it was the work of Robert Denneistoun or Danielstoun, who became a freeman of the Edinburgh Goldsmiths' Incorporation on 23rd April, 1597, and was Deacon of his craft from 1608 to 1610. Attached to the bell by silver chains are twenty-two small silver tablets, bearing the names of various winners—the weight of the bells and tablets being 30 oz. 2 dwt. The oldest tablet is inscribed thus—

> Vin + Be me +
> Sir Iohne +
> Hamilton
> Of + Trabro
> vn + 1628

The others are quite modern, dating between 1852 and 1888. In the year 1661 the bell went amissing, and was not recovered till 1852, when it was found in the repositories of the Lanark Town Council. It was exhibited in the "Sports and Arts Exhibition" of the Grosvenor Gallery, London, in 1890, being then held by Mr. A. H. Laidlay, Edinburgh, the last winner with his horse *Horton*. An engraving and descriptions of the bell appeared in the *Field* of 22nd and 29th March, 1890.

The following Obligation, of date 12th April, 1631, entered in the Town Council books of Stirling, shows that the sport was kept up there, and that the prizes were as yet unchanged :—

In presence of the Provost and Bailies, compeared personally Mr. Thomas

Rollok, younger, burgess of the said burgh of Stirling, and became acted
and obliged of his ain confession, as cautioner and surety for John Drummond of Garnok, that he shall exhibit, present, and deliver to the Provost,
or any one of the Bailies of the said burgh of Stirling, within the said burgh,
upon the first day of March next to come, all and haill these silver bells,
extending to the number of aucht bells, weighing in the haill aucht unce and
nine drape weight, which he wan this day, being Peace Tuesday, at the Bell
Race, to be run again, the next Peace Tuesday, betwixt Bannockburn and
Stirling, and that under the pain of 50 merks money of this realm, to be paid
to the Treasurer of this burgh, to the town's use, in case of failure.

The Palm Sunday race of 1633 at Perth was for a piece
of plate of the value of £40; and the cup of 1637 was
won by Francis Story, servant to Lord Fenton. The
troublous days of the Covenant were now at hand. But
it does not appear that horse-racing was specially proscribed in Scotland during the Covenanting era—although
there could be very little public pastime in a period of
national confusion. Races seem to have been run at
Cupar Fife in April, 1642. That year a charge was
lodged with the criminal authorities by James Stewart of
Ardvoirlich (afterwards the assassin of Montrose's friend,
Lord Kilpont) against Laurence Mercer, son of Sir
Laurence Mercer of Meikleour, and other three students
at St. Andrews, accusing them of having murdered the
complainer's son, Alexander Stewart, in a "tumult
between two classes" of students. The matter was taken
up, and Laurence Mercer and the others were summoned
to appear before the Lords of Privy Council on the 8th
June, 1643. These parties attended; but the Stewarts
failed so to do: and after further procedure, the Council
acquitted Laurence Mercer and his "condisciples" of the
charge, as it was proved that young Ardvoirlich died from
natural causes, and not from the injuries received in the
fight among the students of St. Andrews, the said Alexander having afterwards attended the Cupar Races in

April following, in good health, and there "bursted a poor man's horse" by riding it to death!

"Peebles to the Play!" Although the troubles of the nation were thickening in 1647 and 1648, Peebles kept up its horse-races. The prize was the *Silver Bell* described in the burgh books of those years. On 20th April, 1647, William Jonkesone, younger, burgess of Peebles, became cautioner "for John Stewart, servitor to my lord Earl of Traquair, who having this day received the Silver Bell of Peebles, with two little bells and eight pendicles thereat, that the said John shall re-deliver the same great bell, with the said two little bells, and eight pendicles, together with his ain addition, betwixt and the third day of May next, under the pain of 200 merks Scots money." Next year, on 4th May, "compeared personally ane noble and potent lord, George, Lord Ramsay, who having with ane gray stoned young horse won the Silver Bell of Peebles by running thrice about the stowpes (posts) of Whythauch, has received the said Bell, having appended thereto three little bells and eight pendicles, all weighing ane pound, two ounces, and eleven drop weight of silver," finds caution that the same will be returned on 4th May next year, "with his lordship's addition thereto." *

After the Restoration there was a great revival of Racing in Scotland. The *Mercurius Caledonius*, in March, 1661, advertised the "Race of Haddington," which was to be run on 22nd May, for "a most magnificent cup:" and also that "the Horse race at Lanark, institute by King William above 600 years since, but obstructed these 23 years by the iniquity of the times, is now restored by Sir John

---

* *Charters and Documents relating to the Burgh of Peebles, with Extracts from the Records of the Burgh.* Edinburgh, 1872, p. 382.

Wilkie of Fouldon, as being loathe so ancient a foundation should perish, and for that effect he hath given gratis a piece of plate of the accustomed value, with a silver bell and saddle to the second and third horse : it is to be run the third Tuesday of May." It is suggested in the *Field* that Sir John Wilkie's plate and bell were probably the prizes described as "siller tanker and bell," which were run for in June, 1719. Previously, the Lanark Town Council, on 21st March, that year, appointed "their race for the siller tanker to be run in the usual place upon Thursday, the 14th of June next to come, and the magistrates to be judges in the riding."

In 1661, Horseraces were also held on the Sands of Leith every Saturday ; and at Cupar Fife there was a Race meeting, the prize being a silver cup of the value of £18. Next year, in May, the Dumfries Town Council offered a silver bell of four ounces, to be run for every second Tuesday of May, by the work-horses of the burgh, "according to the ancient custom ; " and if the prize was won by the same horse and rider for three years consecutively, it was to become the property of the winner. Again, in 1664, the Council offered a silver cup of forty ounces, to be run for by noblemen and gentlemen's horses. The Town Council of Stirling, in 1665, 1673, and 1674, offered a silver cup : the course being on the Bridge-haugh, and the time the month of May.

This was probably about the time when the far famed Habbie Simson, Piper of Kilbarchan, blew his enlivening strains at Race-meetings in the west country,—as commemorated by the facetious poet of Beltrees in elegiac verse :—

> " ——At horse races many a day,
> Before the black, the brown, the gray,
> He gart his pipe, when he did play,
>   Baith skirl and screed.

> Now all such pastime's quite away,
> Sin Habbie's dead!"

Some entries in a volume of accounts preserved among the Aberdeen papers at Haddo House, show how the Earl of Aberdeen, who was Chancellor of Scotland from 10th May, 1682, to 21st November, 1684, patronized Leith Races :

1682, July 17. To my lord going to Leith to his race, per Account, £8 8s.
For weighing the men at Leith that rade, £1 8s.
To the man that ran the night before the race, 18s.
Item to the two grooms drink money at winning the race at Leith, £8 8s.
Item to the Edinburgh Officers with the cup, £14.
Item to the Smith boy plaitt the running horse feet, 14s.

Until the Revolution year, 1688, the race at Perth was called "The Bell Race;" but thereafter, by authority of the Magistrates, it was denominated "the race for a cup and other prizes."

At Dunfermline, as we learn from Dr. Henderson's *Annals* of that town, the Town Council, on 16th July, 1702, "ordained the Treasurer to put out a Saddle on the town's account, to be ridden on the morn after July market, betwixt the Town-green and Buckieburn, back and fore ; the input, each horse, £1 10s.; the horse not to be above £5 sterling value ; and ordained the Treasurer also to buy a bonnet and a pair of stockings, to be exposed for a Foot-race on this same ground immediately after the Horse-race, with ribbons to the bonnet." Again, on 4th August, 1707, the Council "warrants the Treasurer to pay the Saddler, £6 for the saddle ridden at July market last."

New attractions for the Race-meetings were provided at Stirling. The Town Council, on 16th April, 1706, "appoints intimation to be made by tuck of drum that there is ane *Goose Race* to be ridden for by the maltmen of this burgh, upon the Saturday immediately before Whitsunday next, a little without the Burrows gate, which is to begin at nine o'clock in the morning : as also ane *Horse Race* for ane new saddle and furniture, to the value of £12. 14s., to be ridden for the said day at one o'clock in the afternoon, betwixt the Burrows gate and William Shirray's in Cambusbarron, back and fore, value of each horse to run not to exceed £60 : as also ane *Foot Race* betwixt the Burrows gate and Whytehill, at three o'clock the same day, for ane pair of stockings, new shoes, and blue bonnet." In the following year there were additions to the programme. The Council, on 21st April, 1707, "appoints ane *Horse Race* to be run at Stirling, upon the   day of May next for ane Silver Mug, to the value of   , which is to bear in great letters 'Stirling Prize :' as also ane *Foot Race* to be run for by Men only, for ane pair of shoes, ane pair of stockings, ane pair of gloves, and ane bonnet : as also recommends to the Guildry to order ane *Race for ane large Gold Ring*, to be run for upon horseback with lances the foresaid day ; and to the Maltmen to appoint ane *Goose Race* the same day ; and the Omnigatherum (the Carters) to appoint another *Race for ane load Saddle*, ane pair of Sods (a sort of saddle used by the lower classes, made of cloth stuffed), and ane new sack full of coals, the same day : and appoints all the foresaid Races to be put in the weekly *Gazette* for six weeks to come, to the effect the lieges may be acquainted therewith." A minute of 21st July following, states the Town's part of the expense of the Races as being £52. 0s. 8d.

The race meetings of 1714 and 1715 are said to have given the Jacobite party in the south of Scotland opportunities for plotting in the interest of the Chevalier de St. George. At the Lochmaben races the plates bore political devices : and on one of these occasions, when the

races were over, a party of the Jacobite gentry went to
the Cross of the burgh, and drank the Pretender's health
on bended knees! In 1720, a variety of race-meetings
at Scottish towns were advertised.   Chambers, in his
Domestic Annals, enumerates—" a race at Cupar in Fife ;
one at Galarig, near Selkirk, for a piece of plate given by
the burgh, of £12 value ; a race at Hamilton Moor for
£10 ; a race on Lanark Moor for a plate of £12, given by
the burgh ; a race on the sands of Leith for a gold cup of
about a hundred guineas value, and another for a plate of
£50 value, given by the city of Edinburgh ; finally,
another race at Leith, for a silver punch-bowl and ladle,
of £25 value, given by the captains of the Trained Bands
of Edinburgh."

The Town Council of Dunfermline, on 26th April, 1723,
" resolved to put out a Saddle for a race to be run on
Wednesday next at two o'clock afternoon : and com-
missioned the two Bailies, the Dean of Guild, and
Treasurer, to buy the Saddle, and draw out the Articles."
Farther, on 30th April, same year, " the Council, for
encouraging of the *Gardeners' Race*, to be kept up here,
they agreed that the town shall next year contribute 30s.
sterling for buying and putting a plate for next year."

At Perth, on 9th September, 1734, the Town Council
agreed to give ten guineas towards making up 75 guineas,
or three purses, for the Horse-races " to be run here next
week."   On 1st July, 1737, the Council agreed to give a
silver plate of £15 value, or that sum in money, to the
races ; and on 27th August, 1738, they agreed to give a
prize of £15. 15s.   At sometime during the century, it
was found convenient to transfer the race-course to the
North Inch ; which, however, was then only half its
present dimensions, being bounded on the north by a
wall called the White Dyke, which the Town Council

ordered to be built on 6th November, 1727, and which ran across from Balhousie Castle to the bank of the Tay, dividing the town's property from that of the Kinnoull family. This wall was erected as a check to the encroachments of the Muirton tacksmen, who, when ploughing their land, occasionally took a furrow or two from the Inch ; and the expense is traditionally (probably erroneously) said to have been defrayed out of the fines imposed on the bakers and brewers of the burgh for fighting with the weavers.

In a Tack, dated 1761, granted by the Town, of the grass and pasturage of the North and South Inches, a clause appears to the effect that " liberty is reserved for the Golf, Archers, and other pastimes, conform to use and wont ; and liberty for the running Horse-races, and for airing and sweating the said horses for three weeks before the week of the Race ; and that the Races be no sooner in the year than September." In 1803, the North Inch was enlarged to its existing size under an excambion with the Earl of Kinnoull ; but, previous to that bargain, the race-course was nearly the same as it is at this day, the Earl permitting it to go through his grounds by temporary openings being made in the boundary wall.

Eventually the annual Races on the Sands of Leith lengthened out until they lasted a week in July or August, being run daily during the recess of the tide. The patrons were the Magistrates of Edinburgh, who marched in procession to the scene every day, attended by the Town Guard ; and the inhabitants of the capital and its seaport kept high holiday throughout the week, affording ample scope for the manners-painting muse of Robert Fergusson, who celebrates " Leith Races " in one of the most characteristic and mirth-provoking of his effusions.

A memorable race was run in January, 1769. Two

country gentlemen, Mr. Maxwell of Dalswinton and Mr. Blair of Dunrod laid a wager of £200 sterling which of them should ride soonest from Dumfries to Kirkcudbright, a distance of about 27 miles. They started; but Mr. Blair became ill on the road, seven miles short of Kirkcudbright, the goal, and yielded the race, giving a Bill for the amount of the wager. He died before the Bill became due. His heir refused payment, and the winner took the matter into the Court of Session. The case was fully argued ; and on 16th December, 1774, the Court gave final judgment, finding that under the Act of James VI. in 1621, cap. 21, all money won at Cards and Dice, or in wagers at Horse-races, above 100 merks Scots, belonged to the poor of the parish.

A year or two after this date—namely in August, 1777 —the *Caledonian Hunt* was instituted at Hamilton House, the original members being twelve in number ; and its turf-meetings lasted a whole week. About 1784, the *Perthshire Hunt* was established by the county gentry, and proved a success. The races on the North Inch, under its auspices, took place in October, also continuing for a week, with ordinaries and balls daily. The palmy days of the Perth Turf saw it as numerously and influentially frequented as any other in Scotland : and when the Caledonian Hunt came thither, according to rotation, the assemblies, it is stated, were prolonged for a fortnight,— the Fair City then becoming the centre of attraction as a resort of fashion.

With the close of the eighteenth century, our discursive task must end, as we are persuaded that the foregoing details really exhaust most of what the general reader may be supposed to reckon curious and interesting in the history of the Scottish Turf. And we will conclude with the judicious remark of a popular sporting writer (" The

Druid," in his *Post and Paddock*) that while believing "that the Turf would sicken and droop without betting, as completely as commerce and business without speculation, we cannot but deeply deplore that men with ample means will not consider such a noble sport quite amusement enough, without the extra stimulant of 'the jingle of the guinea.'"

CHAPTER VII.

ARCHERY—FOOTBALL—GOLF.

Now like themselves again the archers raise
The Bow, in brave array, and claim our lays.
Allan Ramsay.

——Some, with many a merry shout,
In riot, revelry, and rout,
    Pursued the foot-ball play.
Lay of the Last Minstrel.

It is, indeed, a goodly sight to see
Those red-coat champions marshalled for the fray,
Driving the ball o'er bunker, rut, and lea,
And clearing, with impetuous " hove," the way,
Enlivening still the game with laugh and say,
Whilst trotting club-men follow fast behind,
Prepared with ready hand the *tees* to lay,
With nicest eye the devious ball to find,
And of the going game each player to remind.
Lines on Golf.

I.—ARCHERY.

WHILST the Scottish Government was hounding out the peasantry to the wolf-hunt, it was waging war against the popular pastimes of football and golf. The crusade was instigated by the highest patriotic motives. During their oft-renewed strife with England,

the Scots found good cause to dread the superiority of
their " auld enemies " in the use of the long bow ; and yet
this was a weapon which the Lowland infantry persistently
neglected for the spear. It was the terribly-incessant
" arrowy shower " of the English that routed the Scottish
army at Halidon Hill—a scene of ruin and death which
the dramatic page of Sir Walter has so vividly depicted :

> *King Edward.*—See it descending now, the fatal hail-shower,
> The storm of England's wrath—sure, swift, resistless,
> Which no mail-coat can brook. Brave English hearts !
> How close they shoot together ;—as one eye
> Had aim'd five thousand shafts—as if one hand
> Had loosed five thousand bow-strings !
>   *Percy.*—The thick volley
> Darkens the air, and hides the sun from us.

But the Lowland Scots never took kindly to the bow, as
a weapon of warfare ; and history relates what their
huddled masses of spearmen suffered at Flodden, where
" fell England's arrow-flight like rain." In the Highlands,
however, the bow found favour with the Clan-warriors,
who brought it into the field of battle after the middle of
the seventeenth century. According to an Ossianic verse,
the Highland archer could only be properly equipped
with arms the materials of which were thus obtained :

> " Bow of the yew of Essrakin,
>   Feather from the eagle of Lochtreig,
>   Yellow wax of Balenageloin,
>   And an (arrow) head from the smith MacPeteran."

Or, as otherwise stated, the Highland bows were made of
the yews of Glenure, which were esteemed the best for the
purpose ; the shafts were fabricated of the wood of
Esragoin forest, in Lorn, and feathered with the plumage
of the eagle. Highland archers often displayed an accuracy
in transfixing the stag in the height of his headlong

career, which would have done honour to the merry men
of Sherwood. An old narrative of the Battle of Glenlivat
or Balrinnes, which was fought on the 3rd October 1594,
mentions that there were so many archers present that
" at the charge, for the space of a full quarter of an hour,
daylight was palpably eclipsed with the continual cloud
of darts and arrows that hung over the place, the same as
Lucan reports of the battle of Pharsalia."*

When Charles I. was mustering soldiers for the French
war, in 1627, he requested the Laird of Glenurchy, Black
Duncan of the Cowl, to assist in levying a body of 200
Celtic archers, having heard great praise of their skill. At
that time, a strong body of Highland bowmen, commanded
by Alexander M'Naughton of that Ilk, and accompanied
by a number of the Clan Mackinnon, with harpers and
pipers, embarked for France to bear part in the war.
Again, when the same monarch visited Scotland, for his
coronation, in June 1633, a Missive was despatched by the
Scottish Privy Council, on the 29th of that month, to
Black Duncan's son, Sir Colin, in reference to his Majesty's
intended progress to Perth, which city he entered, in royal
state, on the 8th July. "Whereas," said the letter, "the
King's Majesty is most solicit and desirous that the time
of his being at Perth there may be a show and muster
of Highlandmen, in their country habit and best order; for
the better performance whereof, these are to entreat and
desire you to single out and convene a number of your
friends, followers, and depenmembers, men personable for
stature, and in their best array and equipage, with trews,
bows, dorlochs (dirks), and others their ordinary weapons
and furniture, and to send them to the said burgh of Perth
upon Monday the 8th day of July next, whereby his

---

* The Spottiswoode Miscellany, vol. i., p. 267.

Majesty may receive contentment, the country credit, and yourself thanks." It is to be presumed that the party of tartaned archers duly appeared at the pageants in the Fair City.

At the commencement of the Civil War in England, the Earl of Essex issued a precept, dated in November 1643, for stirring up all well-affected people by benevolence towards the raising of a company of archers for the service of Parliament. "Nothing doubting," he said, "but that success will attend the use of that honourable and ancient weapon," the bow, "heretofore found of good use in this kingdom." But it is believed that the last time Archers appeared in English warfare was in September 1645, at the last siege of Devizes by the Parliamentarians. In Scotland, the slender force with which Montrose won the battle of Tibbermuir included a body of Highland archers; and doubtless the bow played its part on the other fields of his fame. It was used in a conflict between the Clans of Breadalbane and Glencoe, after the Restoration: and about 1664, Lochiel had 300 archers in the battle which he fought with the Macintoshes. So much for the Highland archery.

In the fifteenth century the Scottish Government strove with commendable energy to promote the toxophilite art amongst the people; and as the Lowlanders were passionately fond of football and golf, it was determined to suppress these sports in the interest of the valued bow. Here, again, England afforded a precedent—Edward III. having issued an edict in 1349 prohibitory of football and some other amusements, with a similar purpose in view. Accordingly, in 1424, when James I. had just returned from his captivity at Windsor, a statute was passed, enacting that " Na man play at the fute-ball, under the paine of fiftie shillings ; " and another that " all men busk

them to be archers fra they be twelve yeir of age," under
the penalty of "a wedder a man," and that bow-butts or
targets be set up beside every parish kirk. The young
monarch, richly endowed with poetic genius, invoked the
powers of satire in support of law ; and his poem of
" Christ's Kirk on the Green " ridicules with great force
of humour the unskilfulness of his subjects in shooting
with the bow.

James II., in 1457, instituted provincial military
musters, called Weaponschawings, and the universal
practice of archery, and ordered " that the fute-ball and
golfe be utterly cried downe and not to be used." Again,
in 1491, James IV. denounced " fute-ball, golfe, or other
sik unprofitable sports," and renewed the previous acts in
favour of archery. Despite, however, the national importance of the object, the Lowland Scots were very slack in
their obedience. Yet, in the year 1534, at a match
between several Scottish and English bowmen, the former
bore the bell ! This event is detailed with great precision
by Lindsay of Pitscottie. The Lord William Howard
had reached Scotland, as envoy from Henry VIII.,
bringing with him the Order of the Garter with which to
invest James V. who was then two and twenty. In
Howard's train were three-score horsemen, " wailled," or
picked, " gentlemen for all kind of pastime, at shooting,
leaping, wrestling, running, and casting of the stone."
The Scots competed with, and almost invariably beat
them, which so highly mortified King Henry's sister,
Margaret, the Queen Dowager of Scotland, who was a
votaress of the bow herself, that she gave a special chance
to her countrymen of redeeming their honour as archers.
" She took ane wager of archery upon the Englishmen's
hands," says Pitscottie, " contrair (against) the King her
son, and any half-dozen Scotsmen, either noblemen,

gentlemen, or yeomen, that so many Englishmen should shoot against them at rovers, butts, or prick-bonnet. The King, hearing of this bonspiel of his mother, was well content. So there was laid an hundred crowns and ane tun of wine pandit (pledged) on every side. The ground was chosen in St. Andrews. The Scots archers was three landed gentlemen and three yeomen, to wit, David Wemyss of that Ilk, David Arnott of that Ilk, and Mr. John Wedderburn, vicar of Dundee : the yeomen was John Thomson in Leith, Stephen Tabroner, and Alexander Baillie, who was ane piper ; and (they) shot wondrous near, and won the wager from the Englishmen ; and thereafter went into the town, and made a banquet to the King and the Queen, and the English Ambassador, with the whole two hundred crowns and the two tuns of wine. Albeit that the Englishmen confessed that the Scotsmen should have been freed of the payment of that banquet, which was so gorgeous that it was of no less avail (value) than the said gold and wine extended to."[*]

Strangely enough, at the very juncture when fire-arms were beginning to change the whole system of warfare, the English government evinced much anxiety for the encouragement of archery, and resuscitated the old mandates against games supposed to be inimical thereto. Moreover, it was in 1545, that Roger Ascham published his *Toxophilus*, arguing " that styll, according to the oulde wont of England, youth should use " the bow "for the most honest pastyme in peace, that men myght handle it as a moost sure weapon in warre." But we need not smile at Ascham's advocacy of what the musket was fast relegating to the category of the obsolete in military equipment, when we find a notable general of last century

---

—John, Earl of Craufurd—gravely recommending the adoption of archery in the British army as "an advantage to these nations, for, in the former wars between France and England, the English had generally the superiority, chiefly by their being stronger men, and better skilled in archery."*

Franklin, too, advocated the same thing, in a letter to Major General Lee, dated 11th February, 1776, upon six reasons :—

1. Because a man may shoot as truly with a bow as with a common musket.

2. He can discharge four arrows in the time of charging and discharging one bullet.

3. His object is not taken from his view by the smoke of his own side.

4. A flight of arrows seen coming upon them terrifies and disturbs the enemy's attention to his business.

5. An arrow sticking in any part of a man, puts him *hors de combat* till it is extracted.

6. Bows and arrows are more easily provided everywhere than muskets and ammunition.

Further, Moore tells us that the ill-fated Lord Edward Fitzgerald had a notion that for the purpose of training troops to be good marksmen, fire-arms might be dispensed with, and the expense of ammunition which target-practice required be saved. "Having observed, while in America, that the Indians, who are almost all expert marksmen, have obtained this accuracy of aim by the use of the bow and arrow while young, he was of opinion that among the means of training a people to national warfare, the same economical practice might be adopted,—the habit of aiming at a mark with any missile, whether bow or sling, being sure to establish that sort of sympathy between the

---

* Richard Rolt's Memoirs of John Lindesay, Earl of Craufurd and Lindesay, 1753, p. 431.

hand and eye which enables the execution of the one to follow instantly the direction of the other, and this precision of aim once acquired, being, with little difficulty, transferable to the use of the musket or rifle." The biographer adds, however, that it was "somewhat questionable" whether Lord Edward had any "serious notions" of adopting such a suggestion "in his system of military organization for Ireland."*

The statutes for the promotion of archery may have habituated the Low-country Scots to the use of the bow; but the weapon being seemingly unadapted to their military genius, they, in general, never attained such proficiency with it in the battle-field as distinguished the countrymen of Robin Hood and Little John, yet after its supersedence in warfare, it was voluntarily retained throughout Scotland for purposes of recreation. It was much in vogue, during the earlier years of the seventeenth century, among the better classes of society: and King James' Declaration of Sports, which was promulgated at Edinburgh in June, 1618, included archery among the "lawful recreations of the people" on Sundays. In this way the bow-butts, which had been set up at every rural parish kirk and in the green fields adjoining the towns, still continued serviceable. The civic authorities of Perth had formerly appropriated for the toxopholite exercises of the citizens, an ample area of ground, lying on the west of the city, and called indifferently the Bow-butts and the Playfield. But afterwards a portion of the lands on the north side of the town, once belonging to the Dominican Monastery, was forcibly acquired for the like uses. During a considerable period the citizens of Perth appear to have been very fond of archery, and ultimately their principal

---

* Moore's Life of Lord Edward Fitzgerald.

butts were in the South Inch. The local poet, Henry Adamson, in his *Muses Threnodie*, a metrical history of Perth, published posthumously in 1638, makes one of his interlocutors, old George Ruthven, the physician, lament the recent decline of archery in the Fair City, which had once been highly renowned by the feats of her sons.

> How can I choose but mourne? when I think on
> Our games Olympic-like in times agone.
> Chiefly wherein our cunning we did try,
> And matchless skill in noble archerie.
> In these our days when archers did abound
> In Perth, then famous for such pastimes found :
> Among the first, for archers we were known,
> And for that art our skill was loudly blown :
> What time Perth's credit did stand with the best
> And bravest archers this land hath possesst.
> We spar'd nor gaines nor paines for to report
> To *Perth* the worship, by such noble sport ;
> Witness the links of *Leith*, where *Cowper, Grahame,*
> And *Stewart* won the prize, and brought it home ;
> And in these games did offer ten to three,
> There to contend : *Quorum pars magna fui.*

The butts in the South Inch proved, a temptation to Sabbath-breakers—and the Kirk-Session record shows how, on one occasion in 1589, when the ports were closed, in time of sermon, a keen archer clambered over the wall of the Greyfriars Burying ground to get into the Inch for his pastime. The distance betwixt the butts is said to have measured above 500 fathoms ! The young boys of the Fair City seem to have been regularly trained to archery ; for the Town Council, in 1624, issued an order concerning "children going about weekly with their bows and arrows, as use and wont."

The students of Edinburgh University did not neglect the bow. About the end of the sixteenth century, the City Magistrates agreed to "repair the bounds of Mure

Lands," now called Warrender Place, for the practice of archery ; and on the 4th July, 1673, the Treasurer of the College received orders from the Town Council to put up, at the town's expense, " a pair of butts in the College for the Colleginers' recreation." More will be said about Edinburgh archery in the sequel.

At Stirling, the toxopholite art was long held in estimation, but seems to have declined for some time until the last quarter of the seventeenth century. On the 15th April, 1676, " the Magistrates and Council received ane Supplication under the hand of Captain Robert Johnston and other gentlemen, Archers within the said burgh, mentioning that the sport of Archery was almost decayed within this kingdom, yet that other royal burghs were rediviving the same again, humbly entreating therefore that the said Magistrates and Council would give out ane Prize to be shot for, as they should think fit : which Supplication being considered by the said Magistrates and Council, they ordain ane Prize to be shot for to the value of £24. Scots, yearly, during their pleasure, and the time of the shooting therefor to be appointed by them." In 1678, they gave a silver arrow, value £24. Scots ; and in 1679, 1680, and 1681, a silver bow and arrow of the same value.

Kilwinning, an ancient burgh of the west, famous in the annals of Scottish Masonry, is equally famous in those of Scottish Archery. From about 1483, Kilwinning began to hold an annual meeting for competition with the bow. Every year in June the archers assembled for " Shooting at the Papingo "—a wooden painted parrot stuck on the end of a pole, and placed 120 feet high on the bartisan of the Kirk. He who struck this mark was honoured with the title of " Captain of the Papingo " for a year, and latterly had his name inscribed on a medal

which was then attached to a silver arrow. The reader
of Virgil will remember that at the funeral games
instituted by Æneas, when in Sicily, to celebrate his
father's memory, the archers contended by shooting at a
pigeon tied on the top of a mast.

> —————————Æneas orders, for the close,
> The strife of archers with contending bows.
> The mast, Sergesthus' shatter'd galley bore,
> With his own hand he raises on the shore :
> A flutt'ring dove upon the top they tie,
> The living mark at which their arrows fly.

One of the archers who missed—

> —— Miss'd so narrow, that he cut the cord
> Which fasten'd by the foot the flutt'ring bird.
> The captive thus releas'd, away she flies,
> And beats with clapping wings the yielding skies.

But another Sagittarius, more skilful, brought down the
dove as she flew. Thus, the Hurlingham pigeon-shooters
can plead classic precedent for their "sport." At Kilwinning, till 1688, the prize was a sash of parti-coloured
Persian ; but that year a piece of plate was substituted ;
and this again gave way, in 1723, to a silver arrow. The
387th anniversary of these ancient sports was celebrated
in 1870.

The parishioners of Rattray, in eastern Perthshire,
formerly possessed a silver arrow, which was said to have
been gifted by James VI, as a prize at the butts. It was
last shot for in 1727, when it was won by Lord Nairn ;
and on the 22nd of August that year, his Lordship
granted a bond, binding himself to produce the said arrow
with its four tablets appended, if it should be required by
a challenge, and that if no challenge was given within
three months, he should then deliver the arrow to the

keeping of the principal heritor of the parish. The trophy has since been lost.*

At the Bow-butts of St. Andrews, the local archers held competitions from 1618 to 1751. The prizes were three silver arrows, and the winners' names were engraved on silver medals attached. These relics are still shown among the curiosities of the University. The great Marquis of Montrose, while studying at St. Andrews, gained an archery prize in 1628, and his medal, bearing his inscription, still hangs at the second arrow. Subsequently the same arrow was gained by his fellow-student and future rival, the Marquis of Argyle. The sports fell into abeyance during the national convulsions, but were revived after the Restoration. At an archery match in 1687, Mungo Graham, the Laird of Gorthy (Perthshire), won the second arrow ; and his medal was attached to the prize, inscribed with his name and armorial device, the crest of the latter being the two arms and hands of a man holding up a human skull, encircled with two branches of a palm-tree, and over the head the coronet of a Marquis—the motto being *Sepulto viresco* (I grow green when buried). This crest recalls the incident of Gorthy's grandfather having removed Montrose's head from the spike of Edinburgh Tolbooth.† The latest medal on the third arrow is that of the Earl of Elgin, 1751. A number of gentlemen revived the old sport in 1833 ; but finding scant encouragement, their association broke up after a few years. Their arrow is also preserved in the College.

The burgh of Peebles has a silver arrow, which seems

---

* *A Handbook to Blairgowrie, Rattray, and Neighbourhood,* p. 109.

† The medal is engraved in the present writer's *Sketches of the Olden Times in Perthshire.*

to have been decorated with green ribbons on the day of competition, and its oldest medal is dated 1628. The Burgh Accounts between the years 1627 and 1629 contain the following curious entries :—

1628.

June 30. Given to Patrick Waitch, his wife, for wine and ale, and to others, when the Laird of Corcestorffing men shot at the Silver Arrow, -   -   -   -   46s.

August 8. Given at command of the Provost to Mr. John Drowmont that he had depursit in wairing of the Silver Arrow to the Goldsmith, -   -   - £4 17 0

,,   24. Given for three ells of green ribbons to the Silver Arrow before the Provost,-   -   -   -   13s.

,,   26. Given when the Laird of Corcestorffing and his men came to shoot at the Silver Arrow, in the month of October, paid to Patrick Waich, his wife, for wine and ale, -   -   -   -   -   -   - £3 12 8

,,   ,, To Cristiane Hay for ale and tobacco, -   -   -   30s.

,,   ,, In the Provost's house with Corcestorpheine, twa pints wine, -   -   -   -   -   -   30s.

Alhallowmas 1628 to Alhallowmas 1629 :--

To James Haddane, for mending the Bow-butts at Beltane, -   -   -   -   -   -   30s.

In the Provost, his house, when the Silver Arrow shot at St. Peter's Day, -   -   -   -   36s.*

The Peebles arrow was lost from 1675 till 1780, when it was found concealed in the wall of the old Council-house. The silver arrow of Selkirk was also lost from 1674 till 1818.

About the time when Edinburgh College got the "pair of butts" (namely, in 1673), archery was rising into great popularity in the Scottish capital. Many noblemen and gentlemen formed a company of archers, which in 1677 was honoured with the recognition of the Scottish Privy Council, who also gave £20 to procure a prize for compe-

---

* Charters and Documents relating to the Burgh of Peebles, p. 415.

tition. The Marquis of Athole was Captain General of the Company, and the meetings were frequent until the Revolution, when an interval of some years ensued. But the accession of Queen Anne inspired the Society with new life. In 1703, they obtained a Charter under the great seal constituting them as the " Royal Company of Scottish Archers," reviving, in their behalf, the old laws in favour of archery, empowering them to appoint their commanding officers, "and to meet and go forth under their officers' conduct in military form, in manner of weapon-shawing, as often as they should think convenient," and prohibiting the civil magistrate from giving them any interruption ; which rights and privileges they were to hold in free blench of Her Majesty and her successors, paying therefor an annual acknowledgment of a pair of barbed arrows. The membership was wholly composed of Jacobites, and it is very probable that the party aimed at forming, " under a pretext of sports and recreations, a military corps, which, as occasion offered, might assemble under authority of law," and be ready to support the interest of the Chevalier de St. George. In fact, the Company did not hesitate to engross in their Minute-Book a declaration that they remembered, on his birthday, an exiled prince ! Their first military parade was in 1714, when the illness of Queen Anne and the dissensions of the Ministry excited the hopes and fears of political parties to the highest pitch. The Company's uniform was tartan, lined with white, and trimmed with green and white ribbons ; a white sash, with green tassels ; and a blue bonnet, with a St. Andrew's Cross. They carried two standards fluttering in the breeze. The first bore, on one side, Mars and Cupid encircled in a wreath of thistles, with this motto—" *In peace and war :* " and on the other, a yew tree with two archers, encircled as before, and the motto—"*Dat gloria vires.*" The second flag displayed, on one side, the lion rampant, *gules*, on a field *or*, encircled with a wreath, surmounted by a thistle and crown, with the motto—"*Nemo me impune lacesset;*" and on the other, St. Andrew and his cross, on a field *argent*, and at the top a crown, with the motto—"*Dulce pro patria periculam.*" About fifty noblemen and gentlemen, under the aged Earl of Cromarty, marched in array to Leith Links, and there competed for their prize. But the accession of the family of Hanover and the failure of Mar's rebellion damped the ardour of the Archers, and they had no parade for the next nine years. After the insurrection of 1715, the officers of State regarded the Society with so much suspicion that their meetings were watched by spies. The Archers, in course of time, had three prizes: 1st, a silver arrow given by the town of Musselburgh, and to which medals were hung: 2nd, a silver arrow, presented by the city of Edinburgh in 1709: and 3rd, a punch-bowl, said to be of Scottish silver, valued at £50, which was made at the cost of the Company about 1720.* The Musselburgh arrow was first gained by the Earl of Haddington, but the records of the burgh do not mention the year. The first year specified in the books is 1601, since which the arrow was contended for annually, with few exceptions, during the seventeenth and eighteenth centuries and more — the Magistrates of Musselburgh being in the habit of presenting the Company on each occasion with as much claret as could be carried on a coal riddle : and in 1679, the Magistrates, to obtain a fuller attendance of the Company than had become usual, agreed to present the successful competitor that year with a silver bowl in the form of a mussel-shell.†

---

* Arnot's *History of Edinburgh.*
† *Edinburgh Annual Register for 1810*, p. 147.

And we must not forget that Allan Ramsay, the poet, was a warm admirer of a body whose political leanings coincided with his own, and frequently attuned his lyre in praise of the Archers.

Most likely on account of being involved in the odium of Jacobitism, the Society fell into a declining state for many years, until, the old leaven having been purged out by the utter extinguishment of all hope of a Stuart restoration, a better era opened. In 1776, the Company, then consisting of about 300 members, built a hall, near the Meadows, for their meetings, at the cost of £1200. But we must pass rapidly over their subsequent history. In 1822, when George IV. visited Edinburgh, the Archers acted as the royal body-guard : and the King gave them a dress uniform, and conferred on their Captain-General a gold stick. In terms of their charter, they delivered to His Majesty through the Earl of Hopetoun, their Captain-General, a pair of barbed arrows—the shafts being composed of snakewood and the barbs of silver—each bearing the inscription, " To His Majesty King George IV. Reddendo of Royal Company of Archers. Holyrood, August, 1822." When William IV. came to the throne, the Captain-General received a gold stick, the two officers next in command a silver stick each, and the Councillors ebony sticks. The uniform was also changed : and in 1832 the King sent down a splendid pair of colours. The Archers again acted as the body-guard of royalty when Queen Victoria came to Edinburgh in 1842. To this day the Archers form one of the old institutions of the " grey metropolis of the North."

The bow, our readers will smile to be told, has been pressed into the service of the duellist. An Edinburgh paper of the time has recorded that on the 10th of February, 1791, two gentlemen met in the Meadows there, equipped with bows and arrows, to decide a point of honour. They were accompanied by seconds, and had a surgeon in attendance, in case their Indian artillery should by any chance prove effective. After a harmless exchange of three shots, the parties retired, the point of honour, doubtless, being thus satisfactorily arranged. If (remarks the writer) similar weapons were always employed in duelling, this amusement would speedily become unfashionable, seeing that the seconds would run quite as great, if not a greater, risk, than the principals.

After the general disuse of the bow in war, King James VI., about 1617, presented a toy silver gun to the town of Dumfries, which the Seven Trades of the burgh were to compete for annually with the musket. This gun is a silver tube, like the barrel of a pistol, and about ten inches long. It has standard marks stamped on it, and according to tradition was originally mounted on a carriage with wheels, all of silver ; but of these no vestige remains. Near the touch-hole the letters I·M are engraved on the barrel, supposed to be the initials of the Provost of Dumfries at the time when this ceremony was first instituted. This, however, is mere conjecture : such records of the Corporations as were prior to the reign of Charles I. have suffered so much by decay, that they are no longer legible ; and after that period, the only mention of the *Silver Gun* in them is an occasional memorandum of its having been shot for " agreeably to the institution." The royal donor's behest was observed, with general punctuality, for nearly two centuries ; and throughout the long reign of George III. the prize was invariably shot for, on the 4th of June, being the King's birthday. John Mayne's poem of *The Siller Gun*, which will be freshly remembered by all lovers of Scottish poetry, embodies a

laughter-moving picture of the meeting and its worthies
a century back :—

> " For loyal feats, and trophies won,
>   Dumfries shall live till time be done !
>   Ae simmer's morning, wi' the sun,
>   The Seven Trades there,
>   Forgather'd, for their Siller Gun
>   To shoot ance mair ! "
>
>   .   .   .   .   .   .

After many blunders and mischances of a host of competitors, the prize was finally won by William M'Nish, a
Knight of the Thimble.

> " His winsome wife, wha lang had miss'd him,
>   Press'd through the crowd, caress'd and kiss'd him :
>   Less furthy dames (who could resist them ?)
>   Th' example take ;
>   And some held up his bairns, and bless'd them,
>   For daddy's sake !
>
>   In William's hat, wi' ribbons bound,
>   The Gunny was wi' laurel crowned ;
>   And, while in triumph ower the ground
>   They bore him tenty,
>   His health in streams o' punch gaed round,
>   ' Lang life and plenty ! '
>
>   Wi' loud applause, frae man and woman,
>   His fame spread like a spate wide foamin' !
>   Warse deeds hae gi'en to mony a Roman
>   Immortal fame ;
>   But prodigies are grown sae common,
>   They've tint the name ! "

The Notes to the poem state further that the silver
gun is at all times deposited among the archives of the
Dumfries Corporations. When a day was fixed and a
mandate issued for the gathering, all the freemen of the
Trades were obliged to appear in arms at the time and
place appointed by the Convener. If any individual re-

fused to appear, he was subjected to a fine of £40 Scots, equal to £3 6s. 8d. sterling, and till payment thereof, interdicted from voting in any of the Corporation affairs. But for a long time the "gunny" has lain undisturbed in its repository.

A similar prize belongs to the burgh of Kirkcudbright, and is said to have been the gift of James VI. to the Corporations of that place. It is about seven inches long, and marked "T * M.C * 1587 ;" which letters are supposed to be the initials of Sir Thomas M'Clellan, Laird of Bombie, and Provost of Kirkcudbright in 1587. The last competition is said to have been in the summer of 1781.

II.—FOOTBALL.

Acts of Parliament failed to put down the proscribed games of Football and Golf in Scotland. We have seen that James IV., in 1491, denounced both games, "or other such unprofitable sports," yet we find the same monarch's precept and example, in that respect, sadly at variance ; for the Lord High Treasurer notes in his Accounts, on 22nd April, 1497 :—"Item, given to James Dog to buy *footballs to the King*, 2s." Previous to the Reformation, Football was a Sunday sport, which even ecclesiastics joined in—the Parson in Sir David Lyndsay's *Satire of the Three Estates* being made to boast—

> " Though I preach not, I can play at the *caiche* :
> I wot there is not ane amang you all
> Mair feirlie can play at the *Foot-ball*."

Even after the Reformation, the Kirk was frequently scandalized by football-playing, in various quarters, on the Sabbath. Thus, we find from the Perth Kirk Session Records that, in February, 1591-2, about a dozen of men, with the heir of Luncarty at the head of them, confessed "that on the Sunday of the Fast, in time of preaching, afternoon, they were playing at football in the Meadow Inch of the Muirton," a little north of the city. There are two other instances, preserved by tradition, of the same sort of Sabbath desecration in Perthshire, although of later dates, which may here be adduced :—

It is related that sometime in the seventeenth century, the minister of Blairgowrie was a Mr. John Ross, a gentleman of unwonted muscular strength, which he often exercised in seeking to restrain his parishioners from the evil of their ways, as he was always ready with a cuff or a blow to enforce his precepts and admonitions. The young men of the parish were fond of playing at the football on the Sabbaths, between the forenoon and afternoon diets of worship, heedless of the stern dehortations of their worthy pastor. One Sunday, Mr. Ross suddenly appeared at the beginning of the game, and sticking his staff upright in the ground, divested himself of his coat, which he hung upon it, saying, "Stand you there, as minister o' Blair, while I, John Ross, get a game at the ba !" To the amazement of the players, he immediately mingled in the contest ; but instead of kicking the ball, he struck right and left with his heavy boots, until he sent one fellow after another limping out of the *melee*, and in a few minutes there was nobody in the field to oppose him. Invariably after this, when the minister came to the play-ground, the game was stopped, and in the end Sabbath football was abandoned.*

In the parish of Monzie, "the parishioners were in the practice of assembling upon the Green of Monzie, on the Sabbath mornings, to play at football." On such occa-

* *Rambles in Forfarshire.* By James Myles. Dundee : 1850. (P. 209.)

sions, Mr. William Chalmer, the first Presbyterian minister of the parish after the Revolution, who was ordained in July, 1691, experiencing "great difficulty in inducing his people to attend church, occasionally took part with them in this amusement ; by thus gaining their affections, he prevailed on them to accompany him to the house of prayer, and there listen to his instructions." *

Football was the chief pastime on the Border, where it often occasioned broil and bloodshed amongst its moss-trooping patrons. "Such games," says Pitcairn, in his *Criminal Trials*, "were often taken advantage of for the perpetration of deeds of violence ; at least, they were frequently terminated by violence and bloodshed, through the feuds of neighbouring clans or districts." One Sunday, in the month of June, 1600, Sir John Carmichael of that Ilk, Warden of the Middle Marches of Scotland, was present at a great football match, and on his return home was waylaid and murdered by a party of Armstrongs, who bore him a deadly grudge. On another day, a gathering of the Scottish Borderers, at the town of Kelso, held ostensibly for a friendly game at football, became the prelude to a marauding excursion into England. The mischief attendant on the boisterous game has been aptly characterised in a quatrain preserved in the Maitland MS. :—

> " Brissit brawnis, and broken banes,
>   Strife, discord, and waistit wanis,
>   Crooked in eld, syne halt withal,
>   These are the beauties of the Foot-ball."

And to the same effect speaks old Sir Richard Maitland, in his poem of " Solace in Age " :—

> " When young men comes frae the green,
>   Wha playing at foot-ball had been,
>   Wi' broken spauld ;

> I thank my God I want my e'en,
> And am sae auld."

Football shared in the antipathies of James VI., who thus writes concerning it in his *Basilikon Doron*, which was intended for the instruction of his son, Prince Henry: " I think exercises of the body most commendable to be used by a young Prince, in such honest games and pastimes as may further ability and maintain health. . . . But from this count I debar all rough and violent exercise, as the foot-ball ; meeter for laming, than making able the users thereof." The British Solomon's unfortunate mother evinced no such dislike to the pastime ; for we are told by Sir Francis Knollys, that when, on her flight into England, she stopped at Carlisle, " about twenty of her retinue played at football before her the space of two hours, very strongly, nimbly, and skilfully, without any foul play offered."

In the time of the poet Gay—as we see from his *Trivia ; or, The Art of Walking the Streets of London*— the apprentices of the metropolis, always a roystering and pugnacious fraternity, were in the constant habit of playing at football along the Strand, although there were then open fields in the vicinity to which they could have betaken themselves, instead of confusing and obstructing a great public thoroughfare. But long before Gay's time, the little Scottish burgh of Peebles was annoyed by the game being played in the High Street ; and on 20th December, 1570, " the Bailies, Council, and community ordains that there be na playing at the Foot-ball in the Hie Gait in times coming, under the pain of ilk person funding playing 8s., and cutting of the ball." * Jedburgh also was subjected for a time to the like nuisance, as will be afterwards noticed.

---

* *Charters and Documents relating to the Burgh of Peebles*, p. 324.

As with the Reformation and Covenanting ministers, so with the Commonwealth men, the Football was "cried down." On the 11th March, 1659, the second-year students at the College of Edinburgh venturing to play their usual game on the Burgh-muir, were visited with the pains of discipline. Sir David Hume of Crossrig refusing to submit to punishment, was forthwith expelled. But the speedy Restoration of the "merry monarch" changed all this.

At Rattray, in eastern Perthshire, a game of Ball appears to have been statedly played in the parish churchyard. Among the papers of the Craighall family is an Obligation, dated in 1684, by the four last winners of the Silver Ball and Tablets attached thereto, that they should be forthcoming to any four challengers, six days before the playing in the churchyard of Rattray, also the chief heritor to be Keeper of said Ball, and to be produced under a penalty.*

In a poem evincing much of the broad humour and manners-painting genius of our first James, the Rev. John Skinner, author of "Tullochgorum," commemorates the "Christmas Ba'ing" at Monymusk, Aberdeenshire :—

> " The hurry-burry now began,
>   Was right weel worth the seeing,
>   Wi' routs and raps frae man to man,
>   Some getting, and some gieing ;
>   And a' the tricks of fit and han',
>   That ever was in being ;
>   Sometimes the ba' a yirdlins ran,
>   Sometimes in air was fleeing,
>   Fu' heigh that day.

* *Fourth Report of the Royal Commissioners on Historical Documents*, p. 536.

> Has ne'er in Monymuss been seen
>   Sae mony weel-beft skins :
> Of a' the bawmen there was nane
>   But had twa bleedy shins.
> Wi' strenzied shoulders mony ane
>   Dree'd penance for their sins ;
> And what was warst, scoup'd hame at e'en,
>   May be to hungry inns,
>   And cauld that day."

At the present day, the game of Football has experienced a sudden and extraordinary revival in Scotland ;
but how long the *furore* may last is rather problematical
in times of constant change. *Apropos* of a presentation
of £115 and a gold watch and chain to a football
champion in the Vale of Leven, in the summer of 1890,
the *Christian Leader* remarks that "Scotsmen seem now
in the way of achieving greatness with their feet instead
of their heads."

III.—GOLF.

As with Football, so with Golf, both of which games
were denounced by James IV., we find the royal precept
and example antagonistic ; for the Lord High Treasurer's
Accounts contain the following entry, of date 3rd February, 1503-4 : "Item, to the King, *to play at the golf* with
the Earl of Bothwell, 42s."

It is impossible to say whether Golf was ever popular
throughout the Scottish Lowlands. At all events, it has
been localised time out of mind in those east-coast provinces which alone possess the most suitable ground for
its practice. But there is no reason to consider golf as
being an exclusively Scottish game. It was known, in
some fashion or other, to the ancient Romans. With
them the ball (which was made of leather stuffed with
feathers) was termed *paganica*, because the peasantry

were fond of the amusement. Strutt's researches prove
that golf was played in England long ago, though its
recent revival in that quarter of the island has been taken
for its original introduction.

In the reign of Edward III. the Latin name *cambuca* was applied to
this pastime, and it derived the denomination, no doubt, from the crooked
club or bat with which it was played ; the bat was also called a bandy, from
its being bent, and hence the game itself is frequently written in English
bandy-ball.

It should seem that goff was a fashionable game among the nobility at
the commencement of the seventeenth century, and it was one of the exercises with which Prince Henry, eldest son to James I., occasionally amused
himself, as we learn from the following anecdote recorded by a person who
was present : " At another time playing at goff, a play not unlike to pale-
maille, whilst his schoolmaster stood talking with another, and marked not
his highness warning to stand farther off, the prince thinking he had gone
aside, lifted up his goff club to strike the ball : meantyme one standing by
said to him, ' beware that you hit not master Newton : ' wherewith he
drawing back his hand, said, ' Had I done so, I had but paid my debt.' "

A pastime called stow-ball is frequently mentioned by the writers of the
sixteenth and seventeenth centuries, which, I presume, was a species of goff,
at least it appears to have been played with the same kind of ball. In
Littleton's Latin and English Dictionary, under the word *paganica*, the golf-
ball and the stow-ball are the same.*

Golf seems to have become part of the athletic exercises practised at Scottish parochial schools and colleges
immediately after the Reformation. The fascinating
ecclesiastical diarist, James Melvill, tells us that, at Montrose, in the " happie and golden tyme " of his boyhood—
about 1566—he and his schoolmates " were teached " by
their master " to handle the bow for archerie, the club for
goff, the batons for fencing, also to rin, to swoom, to war-
sell, to preve pratticks, everie ane haiffing his matche and
andagonist bathe in our lessons and play." When he

---

* Strutt's *Sports and Pastimes of the People of England.* (Hone's edition),
p. 102.

went to St. Andrews, he says—" For archerie and goff, I had bow, arrose, glub and bals." In 1627, the young James Graham, afterwards the great Marquis of Montrose, entered as a student in the same university, and soon shone as an adept in golf, archery, etc. His accounts of expenditure comprise many items, such as the following :—

The 19th of May for two Golf balls to my Lord - - -		10 sh :
Item, to James Pett, for furnishing my lord in bows, arrows,		
and clubs that year - - - - - -		7 lib. 10 sh :
Nov. eftirnoon, for my Lord's loss at the Golfe - - -		10 sh :
Item, for balls in the Tennis Court at Leith - - -		16 sh :
Item, for 2 Golf balls, my Lord going to the Golf there -		10 sh :

On 4th April, 1603, James VI. conferred the appointment of " Mr. Fledger, Bower, Club-maker, and Speirmaker to his Hienes, als weill for gayme as weir," on William Mayne, Bower and Burgess of Edinburgh, during all the days of his lifetime. Afterwards, in 1618, his Majesty, " understanding that thair is no small quantitie of gold and silver transported zeirlie out of his Hienes' kingdome of Scotland for bying of golf ballis, usit in that kingdome for recreatioun of his Majestie's subjectis, and his Hienes being earnestlie dealt with by James Melvill, in favours of Williame Bervick and his associate, who onlie makis, or can mak golf ballis within the said kingdome for the present, and were the inbringeris off the said trade thair ; " and seeing that the said three parties undertook " to furnische the said kingdome with better golf ballis, and at ane moir easie rate then have been sauld there these manie zeiris bypast," the king granted them a patent for the native manufacture of these articles for the space of twenty-one years, to the exclusion of all other dealers under the condition that " the saids patentaris exceid not the pryce of four schillingis money of this

realme for everie ane of the saidis golfe ballis as for the
pryce thairof ; " and power was given " to the said James,
by himself, his deputies, and servantis, in his name, to
seirch, seik, and apprehend all sik golf ballis as sal be
maid or sauld within his Hienes said kingdome vtherways
then according to the trew meaning of his Majestie's
grant, and to eschiet the saymn." This letter of patent
is dated at Salisbury, 5th August, 1618.

The Town Council of Aberdeen, on 11th May, 1642,
" grants licence and tollerance to John Dickson of making
Gouff balls within this burgh during the Council's pleasure, and his gude carriage and behaviour allenarly, in
respect there is not such ane tradesman in this burgh, and
that he has produced ane testificate from the town of
Leith of his bygane gude life and conversation amongst
them." *

The Kirk-Session records of Perth bear witness that
Golf had its share with Football and other out-door
games in promoting Sabbath desecration :—

1599, November 19. — John Gardner, James Bowman, Lawrence
Chalmers, and Lawrence Cudbert, young boys, confess that they were
playing at the Golf in the North Inch, in time of the preaching after noon
on the Sabbath.

1604, January 2.—The visitors report that good order was kept the last
Sabbath, except that they found some young boys playing at the gowf in the
North Inch in the time of preaching afternoon, who were warned then by
the officiars to compear before the Session this day.

Kings have been the enemies of golf, and kings have
been its eager patrons. Both Charles I. and James II.
enjoyed the pastime in their Scottish kingdom. During
the former monarch's visit to Edinburgh, in 1641, he frequently played golf on the Links of Leith with his Scot-

* *Extracts from the Council Register of the Burgh of Aberdeen, 1625-1642*
(Scottish Burgh Records Society), p. 286.

tish courtiers, most of whom, though loaded with his favours, were secretly disloyal to his cause. In the middle of a busy game, Charles received news of the outbreak of the Irish Rebellion. The club dropped from his hand, and, calling his coach, he drove back to the city, whence he hastened his departure to the south. James II., while Duke of York, and resident in Holyrood Palace as Royal Commissioner to the Scottish Parliament, wielded the club with apparent zest on the breezy links, and by a show of affability, which was perhaps foreign to his narrow, morose nature, acquired much reputation with the populace. It is said that the Duke, on one occasion, had a match with two English noblemen, for heavy stakes, when he assumed as his partner a poor cobbler, but famous golfer, named John Paterson, along with whom he won the victory. The skilful son of St. Crispin was presented with the full amount of the stakes, which enabled him to build for himself a substantial dwelling-house in the Canongate of Edinburgh, and the celebrated Jacobite wit, Dr. Pitcairn, furnished it with a Latin over-door inscription to perpetuate the owner's name and fame. The *Caledonian Mercury* of April 6, 1724, reported "a solemn match at golf," which was played on Leith Links, for twenty guineas, between the Hon. Alexander Elphinstone, one of the sons of Lord Balmerino (and younger brother of the Lord Balmerino, who lost his head on Tower Hill in 1746), and the notorious Captain John Porteous of the Edinburgh Town Guard. It attracted a very numerous and aristocratic assemblage of spectators, including the Duke of Hamilton and the Earl of Morton. The match was won by Mr. Elphinstone. Ten years thence he fought a duel with a Lieutenant Swift on the same spot, and killed him ; and we know what fate overtook Porteous after the lapse of a dozen of years.

Many eminent Scotsmen have been keen votaries of golf. President Forbes, of Culloden, notes in his Journal of date 1st November, 1728 :—" This day, after a very hard pull, I got the better of my son at the gouf on Musselburgh Links. If he was as good at any other thing as he is at that, there would be some hopes of him." The President was so ardent a golfer that he was known sometimes to take a turn of the Links of Leith in the dead of winter, when they were sheeted with snow and ice. Nor was he singular in his enthusiasm. Stories are told of an "Auld Reekie" wight, who frequently prolonged his rounds of Bruntsfield Links till night overtook him, when he would continue the game, on a circumscribed scale, by the feeble aid of a lantern ; and his neglected spouse strove in vain to shame him home by sending him sometimes his supper and sometimes his nightcap ! It is also related of two Edinburgh devotees of the game, that they used to carry it on, after darkness overtook them, by the expedient of rubbing their balls with phosphorus, until one of the players burned his fingers severely with the hot substance ! Even the fishwives of Fisherrow used to recreate themselves at golf, as well as football, on particular holidays ! Their well-known parish minister, that " shrewd auld carle " (as Sir Walter Scott called him), the Rev. Dr. Carlyle of Inveresk, was a crack golfer in his day, and when in London, in 1758, astonished the Cockneys with his skill. This, as we learn from his *Autobiography*, was on his visit to Garrick's house, in company with Dr. Robertson, John Home, and some other gentlemen.

Garrick was so friendly to John Home, that he gave a dinner to his friends and companions, at his house at Hampton, which he did but seldom. He had told us to bring golf clubs and balls, that we might play at that game at Molesly Hurst. We accordingly set out in good time, six of us in a landau. As we passed through Kensington, the Coldstream Regiment were changing guard, and, on seeing our clubs, they gave us three cheers in honour of a diversion peculiar to Scotland : so much does the remembrance of one's native country dilate the heart, when one has been some time absent. The same sentiment made us open our purses, and give our countrymen wherewithal to drink the " Land o' Cakes." Garrick met us by the way, so impatient he seemed to be for his company.

Immediately after we arrived, we crossed the river to the golfing ground, which was very good. None of the company could play but John Home and myself, and Parson Black, from Aberdeen.

Garrick had built a handsome temple, with a statue of Shakespeare in it, in his lower garden, on the banks of the Thames, which was separated from the upper one by a high-road, under which there was an archway which united the two gardens. Garrick, in compliment to Home, had ordered the wine to be carried to this temple, where we were to drink it, under the shade of the copy of that statue to which Home had addressed his pathetic verses on the rejection of his play. The poet and the actor were equally gay, and well pleased with each other, on this occasion, with much respect on the one hand, and a total oblivion of animosity on the other ; for vanity is a passion that is easy to be entreated, and unites freely with all the best affections. Having observed a green mount in the garden, opposite the archway, I said to our landlord, that while the servants were preparing the collation in the temple, I would surprise him with a stroke at the golf, as I should drive a ball through his archway into the Thames once in three strokes. I had measured the distance with my eye in walking about the garden, and accordingly, at the second stroke, made the ball alight in the mouth of the arch-way, and roll down the green slope into the river. This was so dexterous, that he was quite surprised, and begged the club of me by which such a feat had been performed. We passed a very agreeable afternoon ; and it is hard to say which were happier, the landlord and landlady, or the guests.

In 1810, the Musselburgh Golf Club " resolved to present by subscription a new creel and shawl to the best female golfer who plays on the annual occasion on 1st January next old style (12th January, new), to be intimated to the fish ladies by the officer of the Club. Two of the best Barcelona handkerchiefs to be added to the above premium of the creel."

Of curious matches, one or two examples may be given. We learn from the biographical matter in Kay's

Edinburgh Portraits that "in 1798 bets were taken in the Burgess Golfing Society" of the Scottish metropolis, "that no two members could be found capable of driving a ball over the spire of St. Giles's steeple. The late Mr. Sceales of Leith, and the present Mr. Smellie, printer, were selected to perform this formidable undertaking. They were allowed to use six balls each. The balls passed considerably higher than the weather-cock, and were found nearly opposite the Advocate's Close. The bet was decided early in the morning, the parties taking their station at the south-east corner of Parliament Square. The feat is described as one of easy performance. The required elevation was obtained by a barrel-stave suitably fixed ; and the height of the steeple, which is one hundred and sixty-one feet, together with the distance from the base of the church, were found to be much less than a good stroke of the club." A similar feat was performed in 1828, by driving balls over the Melville Monument in St. Andrew Square, Edinburgh—the height of pillar and statue being 150 feet. In the same year, "Captain Hope challenges Mr. Sanderson," both of the Musselburgh Club, "for a watch, the Captain to shoot with a bow and arrow, and Mr. Sanderson to use a club and ball, he being allowed to tee the ball at every stroke"—which match was easily won by the challenger.

The Edinburgh Company of Golfers was formed, it is believed, before 1744, in which year the city presented them with a silver club, to be played for annually ; and at St. Andrews the first Golfing Society or Club was instituted in 1754.

The recent growth of golf in England has been very remarkable. "Fifteen years ago devotees of the game were comparatively few in South Britain, and those who affected it journeyed in their holidays far afield, to West-

ward Ho! or St. Andrews, or similar centres of the game,
to enjoy themselves. When once watering-places began
to compete with each other in the production of "links"
to enhance their attractions, a run began on the game,
and the north-country monopoly of it became endan-
gered. During the last three or four seasons the spread
has been even more rapid, and for want of better grounds
the meadow and pasture inclosures which adjoin many a
country house that does not boast a literal park, have
been pressed into the service." *

* *The Field*, 18th October, 1890.

CHAPTER VIII.

THE REVELS OF FASTREN'S E'EN.

First comes Candlemas,
    And then the new moon,
And the first Tuesday after that
    Is Fastren's E'en.

                              Old Rhyme.

THE British *Carnival* in days of yore was called *Fastren's E'en*, or *Fasten's E'en*, in Scotland, and *Shrove-tide*, or *Shrove Tuesday*, in England : its particular day being regulated by that on which Easter might fall, according to the rule that Shrove-tide must be the seventh Tuesday before Easter. From what derivation the name *Fastren's E'en* proceeded is doubtful : it may have meant the day before, or eve of the Fast of Lent, or again, the Feast of the martyr-brothers, SS. Faustinius and Jovita, of Brescia, who suffered for the faith by being beheaded in their native city, *circa* 121, under the Roman Emperor Adrian. But it signifies little what was the exact origin of the Scottish designation of Shrove-tide : we know that in the centuries before the Reformation, Fastren's E'en was a holiday of roystering revelry and disport, as the people having shriven or confessed themselves and obtained absolution for their sins, plunged into excess of good cheer and frolic during the

few hours which intervened ere the morrow, *Ash Wednes-
.day*, ushered in the period of abstinence and austerity.

Although certainly not inducing in any degree the
riotous merriment and pastime of the day, yet there was
ever something in the natural season itself tending to in-
spire lightness and gaiety of heart at Fastren's E'en.
For then the reign of "surly Winter" is over : and though
the gloomy king, mantled with mist and cloud, and wear-
ing his icicled diadem, still lingers on the northern mountain tops, whence in oft-recurring gusts of rage he casts
forth his tempests, yet in his lost domains young Spring
has assumed the supremacy, and is breathing life into the
clods of the valley, and calling to resurrection the bright
and beautiful floral children of the Earth.   Already the
Fair Maid of February, Emblem of Purity, the Snowdrop,
smiles in her simple charms on the bleak waste.   Now
awakes an eager chorus from the leafless groves : the buds
are red on the hedges : and winged atoms are dancing in
the genial air of noon, when the west wind comes across
the naked leas with a sough of summer.   And hearken to
the voices of the waters !   Freed of their fetters, which
broke and dissolved away at Spring's magic touch, the
rivers, swelling from bank to brae, roll along in their
majesty, with a tumultuous exultant roar like drunken
laughter, tossing on their bosoms the wrecks of flooded
haughs.   Every woodland brook is full to the brim, and
the hill-burns brawl down furiously to the plains.   Dif-
fused abroad seems a deep sense of relief—of emancipa-
tion.   Storms may burst ; the gathered clouds may pour
their deluges ; and the snow-drift may darken the day ;
but a rejuvenating spirit is at work, and will quickly restore universal Nature to her pristine freshness and love-
liness.   Foliage will clothe the naked boughs, and rustle
joyously in the breezes ; the woods will ring with melody ;

the flowers will bespangle the meads. Yet all will not be restored.   There are vanished treasures of the past which not even the power of Spring can bring back to gladden the heart, and which live only in fond remembrance and unavailing regret.

Nought of the pure influences of the season could have moved the feelings which found delight in the coarse festivity, the barbarous sports, and the Bacchanalian madness of Fastren's E'en.   " The common people," says Sir Walter Scott, describing, in the *Fair Maid of Perth*, the festival as it was held in Perth, when Robert III. was King, " had, throughout the day, toiled and struggled at football ; the nobles and gentry had fought cocks, and hearkened to the wanton music of the minstrel ; while the citizens had gorged themselves upon pancakes fried in lard, and brose, or brewis—the fat broth, that is, in which salted beef had been boiled, poured upon highly-toasted oatmeal, a dish which even now is not ungrateful to simple, old-fashioned Scottish palates.   These were all exercises and festive dishes proper to the holiday.   It was no less a solemnity of the evening, that the devout Catholic should drink as much good ale and wine as he had means to procure ; and, if young and able, that he should dance at the ring, or figure among the morrice-dancers, who in the city of Perth, as elsewhere, wore a peculiarly fantastic garb, and distinguished themselves by their address and activity."   At the Court of James IV. the festival was celebrated with Guizing (masking), Morris-dancing, and Tourneying, as abundantly shewn by the Lord High Treasurer's Accounts.

When the Reformation triumphed in Scotland this holiday, was, of course, abolished along with the other festivals of the Romish Church.   But in some of its fashions and pastimes, Fastren's E'en lived on, notwithstanding the ban of the Kirk. Among the characteristic sports of Shrove-tide, both in England and Scotland, cock-fighting was in high esteem ; and it seems to have been anciently common in English schools. The writer, Fitz-stephen, who died in 1191, speaking of the amusements of London, says that "yearly at Shrove-tide the boys of every school bring fighting-cocks to their masters, and all the forenoon is spent at school to see these cocks fight together." Doubtless the like practice obtained in Scottish schools long before the Reformation, and probably was kept up here and there till the era of the Covenant, when it must have been totally suppressed ; for at the Restoration it was ostentatiously "revived," to the great satisfaction of the Cavaliers. Referring to the Fastren's E'en of 1661, the *Mercurius Caledonius* of Edinburgh records that "our carnival sports are in some measure revived, for, according to the ancient custom, the work was carried on by cock-fighting in the schools, and in the streets, among the vulgar sort, tilting at cocks with fagot-sticks." It may be presumed that the example spread over the country. At the beginning of the eighteenth century the science of cock-fighting was popular among certain classes of the citizens of Edinburgh. In 1702 a cockpit was opened at Leith Links, the prices of admission being 10d. to the front row, 7d. to the second row, and 4d. to the third ; and speedily, says Arnot, in his *History of Edinburgh*, " the passion for cock-fighting was so general among all ranks of the people, that the magistrates " of the city " discharged its being practised on the streets, on account of the disturbances it occasioned." In 1705 Mr. William Machrie, residing in Edinburgh, who had been teaching "the severe and serious, but necessary exercise of the sword," turned his attention to the despicable sport then come into favour, and which he called " as

much an art as the managing of horses for races or for the
field of battle," and published an *Essay* on the subject.
He extolled the cruel diversion to the skies, and earnestly
wished that "village may be engaged against village, city
against city, kingdom against kingdom, nay, the father
against the son, until all the wars in Europe, wherein so
much Christian blood is spilt, be turned into the innocent
pastime" of which he was treating.   Edinburgh continued
to patronise the sport for some time ; but at length the
taste turned, and before the middle of the century, cock-
fighting had died out as one of the public amusements of
the capital.   After a lapse of years, however, it came
again into repute, though happily not for any lengthened
period.   The following notes occur in the "Comparative
View of Edinburgh in 1763, 1783, and 1793," drawn up
by Provost Creech, and inserted in his *Fugitive Pieces :*—

In 1763—There was no such diversion as public cock-fighting in Edinburgh.

In 1783—There were many public cock-fighting matches or *mains*, as they
are technically termed ; and a regular cockpit was built for the accommoda-
tion of this school of gambling and cruelty, where every distinction of rank
and character is levelled.

In 1790—The cockpit continued to be frequented.

But, strangest of all, throughout the eighteenth century,
from its opening to its close, the savage diversion was in
full swing, as an established institution, in most of the
schools in Scotland.   Whenever Fastren's E'en came
round, the schools were transformed into cockpits, and in
various cases the sport was also indulged in at Candlemas.
The boys brought the combatants, and the whole day was
devoted to the sport.   The masters profited by it.   Dues
of 2d. or so were paid them for each bird introduced ;
and besides, the killed birds, and also the *fugies*, namely,
those who proved craven, became their perquisites !

Sometimes the boys were treated to drink at the close of the proceedings! Indeed, in poor parishes, these dues and perquisites were accounted as part of the stated salary of the teacher. Thus, the Rev. John M'Queen, minister of Applecross, Ross-shire, says, in his Statistical Account of that parish, published in 1792, that "the schoolmaster's salary is 200 marks Scotch; he hath no perquisites, but the quarter payments of 1s. 6d. for English scholars, and 2s. 6d. for Latin and arithmetic; and the cock-fight dues, which are equal to one quarter's payment for each scholar." Sir James Macintosh, when at Fortrose School in 1776-77, had this entry in his bill: "To cock-fight dues for 2 years, 2s. 6d. each, 5s." And such rude diversions did not altogether cease at the end of last century, but were practised in different districts for years afterwards. The editions of *Hoyle's Games* of the period included a "Treatise on Game Cocks," with rules and calculations for the fight.

Football and other ball games were prominent amongst the popular amusements of Fastren's E'en. An annual ball-match, on that festival, was held at Scone, between the married men and the bachelors, which gave rise to the old saying—"A's fair at the ba' o' Scone." It is said that this contest had its origin in the chivalric ages. "An Italian," as the story goes, in the Statistical Account of that parish, 1796, "came into this part of the country, challenging all the parishes, under a certain penalty in case of declining his challenge." Every one of the parishes "declined the challenge excepting Scone, which beat the foreigner; and in commemoration of this gallant action the game was instituted," to be played yearly on Shrove Tuesday. The competitors ranged their sides at the old market cross of the village. "A ball was then thrown up, and they played from two o'clock to sunset.

The game was this. He who at any time got the ball into his hands, ran with it till overtaken by one of the opposite party, and then, if he could shake himself loose from those on the opposite side who seized him, he ran on : if not, he threw the ball from him, unless it was wrested from him by the other party ; but no person was allowed to kick it. The object of the married men was to hang it, *i.e.*, to put it three times into a small hole in the moor, the *dool* or limit on the one hand ; that of the bachelors was to drown it, *i.e.*, to dip it three times into a deep place in the river, the limit on the other. The party who could effect either of these objects won the game. But if neither party won, the ball was cut into two equal parts at sunset." It is added that "whilst the custom continued, every man in the parish, the gentry not excepted, was obliged to turn out and support the side to which he belonged ; and the person who neglected to do his part on that occasion was fined ; but the custom being attended with certain inconveniencies, was abolished a few years" previous to 1796. The Fastren's E'en football match at Fisherrow, in the Lothian parish of Inveresk, was between the married and unmarried *fish-women*, and it is recorded that "the former were always victorious." A rural poet, David Anderson, the Apprentice Coppersmith, who published his *Scottish Village* at Aberdeen, in 1808, has a sketch of how the holiday was spent among the country-folks on the banks of the Don :—

> Now *Fasten's Even* comes, sweet rural night,
> Life's sweet reviver, and sweet Spring's delight.
> Blythe ev'ry peasant hails its joyful morn,
> But more for night their gladden'd souls do burn.
>
> .   .   .   .   .   .
>
> The twilight now close on the back of noon
> Comes jovial in, attended by the moon ;
> Then forth the Gamesters' equal parties draw,
> To worst each other, driving balls of straw,

Then to the field, the ball with fury spurns,
All crowding strive, the battle warmly burns
On either side, the eager contest's fir'd,
And each to win the glorious game's inspir'd.
Now scattering whiles, they rage, and run, and push,
Now in a group, fast madd'ning on they rush,
While down the field one party victors go,
Now driven back by some unlucky blow,
Calm whiles it sinks, but loud again begins,
Now warms their blood, then spurns each other's shins.
Till equal games upon each other get,
Then to some dance off cheerfully they set.

On the Border, ball-play on Fastren's E'en has been an old custom. At Hawick, as related in Robert Wilson's *History* of that burgh, " a football was played annually on Fastren's Eve within the town," up to about the year 1769, "the inhabitants who lived on the *West Side* of the water of Slitrig being matched against those who resided on the *East Side* of it. This amusement had a bad tendency in keeping up, and promoting, a species of war or fighting that had been carried on, time out of mind, between the people (principally boys) of East and West divisions of the town. This feud, in which the boys below sixteen years of age were the chief combatants, was fostered by their seniors ; and even parents and masters have been known to encourage their apprentices and children to join in the scene of contention. The youngsters of that period, too, formed themselves into regiments ; had drums, standards, and halberds, and were armed also with stones, clubs, and even swords. These battles were sometimes carried to such a height, that adults were induced to mingle in them. . . . This warlike propensity was fiercest for two or three weeks before and after the playing of the ball on Fastren's-eve."

At Jedburgh and Dunse the yearly ball-play has been kept up to our own times. At Jedburgh the game was originally football, and was pursued along the streets of the town, until the Town Council formally prohibited the sport by the following Minute, dated 11th March, 1704:

The Council, having duly considered that the tossing and throwing up of the football at Fastringe's Evin, within the streets of the burgh, has many times tended to the great prejudice of the inhabitants (who now all call for a discharge thereof), there having been sometimes both old and young near lost their lives thereby: therefore they, with all unanimous advice and consent, discharge the same now and in all time coming, as also the ringing of the watch-bell at that time, with certification of one hundred pounds Scots to all contraveners, besides what are contained in the Acts of Parliament of King James the Sixth and his successors relating thereto, and discharging the same.

After this prohibition, the hand-ball was substituted, and the new play took the place of the old.

But "Dunse dings a'!" In the case of this burgh we have a graphic account of its ball-game in the *Transactions of the Berwickshire Naturalists' Club*, and thence transferred to the pages of the *Scottish Journal of Topography, Antiquities, Traditions, etc.*, for 22nd January 1848, from which we now extract it *in extenso*:

THE GAME OF BALL, AS PLAYED AT DUNSE ON FASTERN'S EVE.

By Mr. Thomas Brown.

As one object of this Club is to examine the antiquities of Berwickshire, a brief notice of the above game may not be unacceptable. Though still kept up, the interest taken in it has greatly decreased, and it may not improbably disappear ere long. It is not so much, therefore, from its present state that a complete description is to be drawn, as from the recollections of the oldest inhabitants. I have only to regret that the details here presented are not more complete.

Fastern's Eve, or, as it is here called, Fastern's E'en, was once almost, if not altogether, a holiday to the inhabitants of Dunse. As in many other parishes, cock-fighting was the principal amusement during the forenoon, and, at one period, it seems to have been in high estimation. The parish school, which was set apart for it, is described as having been sometimes crowded to the door, and the fees collected on the occasion formed a perquisite of some value. It is certainly to the honour of the present generation that this practice has disappeared.

The amusements of the afternoon are both more peculiar and inviting. The game is ball, played in a manner which, if not peculiar to Dunse, is at least not common. Preparations for it used to begin nearly a week before. Three young men were chosen to conduct them, and were called "ba'-men." They met on the Wednesday of the preceding week, to hold, along with their friends, the shaping of the ball, when they paraded the town, accompanied by a drum and fiddle, playing the tune :

> Never let the gree go doon,
> For the gude o' our toon.

In this style they called at the houses of the more respectable inhabitants, danced with the servants, and received contributions.

Till the day itself arrived, their only duties were to collect these contributions and prepare the balls. Three are required for the game, but four are always prepared. The family at Dunse Castle have so liberally supported the practice that it has been customary to leave there one of the balls, which, it is said, are preserved. Of those played with the first is gilt, and called the "*golden* ball" ; the second, from its colour, is called the '*silver* ball' ; the third is spotted.

About eleven o'clock in the forenoon the honour of throwing off the ball was at one time exposed to auction in the churchyard over one of the tombstones. The arrangement of the working classes in Dunse, under the different trades, was at that time more complete than at present ; and it was a subject of considerable competition among them who should have the honour of throwing up the ball. My informant states it, as a very early recollection, that the whip-men (carters) bought it for fifteen shillings—a sum which, making allowance for the difference of the value of money, shews the estimation in which it was held. The children of the Drummelzie family, or of the more respectable families in Dunse itself, have of late enjoyed the honour, but it has not unfrequently been left to the ball-men themselves.

It was from the top of a small building that stood close to the old Town-house that the ball was usually thrown. Since that was taken down, it is simply from the street. About one o'clock the shops are shut, the golden ball is thrown off, and the game begins.

The opposing parties are the married and unmarried men. Their object is not to kick the ball, but to snatch it up and carry it off. This, however, is exceedingly difficult. It is thrown into the middle of the crowd, and whoever happens to gain it, is sure that hundreds will rush on him from every point. The scenes to which this leads are, as may be supposed, exceedingly varied and amusing. At one time the crowd is rolled together in a mass, every individual in which is making the greatest exertions to gain or retain the ball. And should the possessor of it be able to escape or to throw it to any distance, the rush which is made, and the eager pursuit, exhibit a very animated sight. The game of the married men is to carry the ball into the church, the doors of which are set open on the occasion. The unmarried men endeavour to reach any mill in the parish, and put the ball into the hopper.

The contests, though conducted in good humour, are usually very determined, and when the game was in higher estimation than at present, it is said that accidents sometimes happened from the pressure of the crowd.

Though the unmarried men might carry the ball to any mill in the parish, they generally endeavour to reach Clock-mill, about half-a-mile to the west of Dunse. It was once customary, therefore, for a party of their opponents to be stationed before it, and many a hard contest took place there. The parties, however, scarcely met on equal terms. The young men, spent with previous exertion, were no match for these fresh opponents, and it not unfrequently ended in their being plunged in the mill-lade. If, however, in spite of all opposition, the mill-hopper was fairly reached, the game was won. And then came the honours. The miller entertained them with pork and *dumplins ;* and, what was of far more importance, dusted them, especially their hats, with flour. Like the laurel wreaths of other regions, this marked them out for the gaze of their fellow-townsmen.

In this way the three balls are played for successively. The person who succeeds in *kirking* or in *milling*—such are the phrases—the first or golden ball, receives from the ball-men a reward of 1/6, for the second 1/, and for the third 6d.

I have no means of ascertaining the antiquity of this practice. The oldest inhabitant tells us that, ever since they recollect, it has been falling off. It seems, indeed, at one time to have been engaged in with much greater spirit. Whoever did not play was marked, and the inhabitants not unusually assembled next day to inflict punishment. They dragged him forth—carried him down to the Cross, and, as is said, knocked him against it. When one thinks of the population, leaving for one day their laborious occupations, and entering with spirit into the excitement of this game, he would be a stern moralist who would forbid them the enjoyment. But every picture has its darker shades. The evening was generally spent in dancing and drinking. It was remarked, too, that if any private quarrels had arisen, they were one way or other settled and set at rest on Fastern's E'en.

We see that this play closely resembled the " Ba' o' Scone," and has survived it to the present day.

The fashion in which the time-honoured festival was celebrated in Kilmarnock, has been delineated by a poetical son of " auld Killie," John Ramsay, in his *Wood-*

notes of a Wanderer (1848).   Holiday was held in the town.   The performances began with the " water-warks," or fire engine, being brought into the streets and set to play at random.

> Jock Stewart took a pipe's comman',
>   Though for his neck 'twas risky,
> And dealt it roun' wi' heavy han'—
>   Ye're sure it wasna whisky.
> For, had it been, he wad, I ween,
>   Ta'en rather better care o't ;
> Nor by his drouth, to ony mouth
>   Hae had ae drap to spare o't—
>   On that same day.
>
> Out-owre the heighest house's tap
>   He sent the torrents scrievin';
> The curious crowd aye nearer crap
>   To see sic feats achievin'.
> But scarcely had they thickened weel,
>   And got in trim for smilin',
> When round the pipe gaed like an eel,
>   And made a pretty skailin'
>   'Mang them that day.
>
> Now here, now there, he took his mark—
>   Now down, now up, he liftit ;
> And droukit some unto the sark
>   That hadna ane to shift it.
> And aye the callants were as keen
>   To stan' and get a blatter,
> As they had Roman Catholics been,
>   And it a' holy water
>   That fell that day.

When the populace had sufficiently enjoyed these ablutions, they marched in procession, headed by the Town Councillors, with halberdier and drummer, to the outskirts of the burgh, where foot-races were run for suitable prizes. Such was "auld Killie's" Fastren's E'en in the early years of this century.

During last century, the members of the Weaver Incorporation of Perth (a very numerous body) kept Fastren's E'en by partaking of cogs of fat brose in the morning, and assembling at night-fall in the public-house of one of their tenants, where they regaled themselves for hours with the strong and heady " twopenny " ale which he brewed. In such and similar festivities, the Incorporation, it is recorded, " guzzled away their funds."

Finally, in regard to Ball-play, we may add that Colonel Forbes Leslie, in his *Early Races of Scotland* (Vol. I., p. 125), is of opinion that "the playing ball was not originally foot-ball, for no one was allowed to kick it."

CHAPTER IX.

THE RUSTIC SPORTS OF LAMMAS.

———In many a Lowland vale,
These annual revels fill, with simple glee,
The husbandman, and cottar, man and child.
Grahame's " British Georgics."

FROM Fastren's E'en we pass on through the
blythe Spring days, through the " merry month
of May," and the " leafy month of June," and
July, fervid with its own Dog-star: and now, on the
sunny stage of the " varied year " appears gracious
Autumn,

——— Rich arrayed
In garment all of gold, down to the ground,

as seen by the rapt eye of the poet of Faerie, and leading

——— a lovely maid
Forth by the lily hand, the which is crown'd
With ears of corn, and full her hand is found.

How changed is the face of Nature since those bracing
Spring days when, under grey, windy skies, the seed was
sown in the brown tilth, scarcely freed from Winter's icy
fetters ! The cultured fields, lately so green, have put on
a mellowness betokening the maturity of the year. The

spikey grain rustles, and shakes heavily, and rolls in billows, at the west wind's will. The woods display dense masses of foliage, darker in hue than when the May breezes fanned the fresh leaves. Many of the summer flowers still linger in the parterre ; but the fairest of the wild-flowers have vanished from their accustomed haunts: the scythe has been busy among the garish grasses : the down of the thistle floats on the sultry air : the young haws supplant the fragrant blossoms of the thorn : the orchards are burdened with the ripening fruit, instead of the snowy flush of May : and the music of the groves has lost its sweetest voices. Soon will the shortening day bring the yellow harvest moon : and soon shall we see the sickle glittering on the "bonny corn rigs," and the rigs of barley, and hear the mirth of the harvest-home. Yet amid the pervading happiness inspired by peace and plenty, Autumn teaches its solemn lessons. Now it is that the heart of man is specially called to pour forth thanksgivings to the beneficent Creator Who crowns the year with His goodness, and whose paths drop fatness. Moreover, harvest scenes have a peculiar association with incidents and images frequent in Sacred Writ. We are reminded of Joseph's dream that he and his jealous brethren were binding sheaves in the field, and, lo ! his sheaf arose, and also stood upright, and, behold, their sheaves stood round about, and made obeisance to his sheaf. We see the fair, devoted Moabitess gleaning in the fields of Naomi's kinsman, and the young men letting fall some of the handfuls of purpose for her. We feel, as it were, the rapture of that good day when the Ark of God was sent back by the Philistines : "and they of Bethshemesh were reaping their wheat-harvest in the valley : and they lifted up their eyes, and saw the ark, and rejoiced to see it." We think of the disciples pluck-

ing the ears of corn by the wayside, and rubbing them in
their hands: of the vision in Patmos, when the banished
saint heard an angel crying with a loud voice to him that
sat on the cloud—"Thrust in thy sickle, and reap; for
the time is come for thee to reap; for the harvest of the
earth is ripe": and of the fine figure of the death of the
righteous man, who goeth to his grave, like a shock of
corn in due season. But there is an unceasing harvest
reaped by Death, whose sickle is ever busy, cutting
down ripe and unripe alike to await in the dust that final
day,

> When the Archangel's blast
> Shall winnow, like a fan, the chaff and grain.

For our life is a progression, and upon all Creation's
charms the immutable truth is impressed that beyond the
bloom of Spring, the glories of Summer, and the fulness
of Autumn, hoary Winter stands at the open portal that
leads to Eternity. "All things have their seasons," says
Seneca; "they begin, they increase, and they die. The
heavens and the earth grow old, and are appointed their
periods. That which we call *death*, is but a pause, or
suspension; and in truth a progress to life; only our
thoughts look downward upon the body, and not forward
upon things to come."

The first day of August, it is believed, was held as one
of the great annual festivals of heathen times in Britain,
being the feast of thanksgiving for the ingathering of the
grain harvest. Hence the term *Gule of August*—the
British or Celtic word, *Gwyl*, signifying a festival or holiday. The same day is set apart in the Romish calendar
as *Festum Sancti Petri ad Vincula*—the Feast of St.
Peter's Chains: and it was also the day when, during the
Papal ascendancy, the English people paid their "Peter's
pence" to Rome. But no connection can be fairly

assumed between the words *Vincula* and *Gwyl*, although
it is very probable that in early days the Pagan festival
received a Christian name and meaning, because the
attachment of the people prevented its abolition. It is
evident, however, that the name *Lammas*, as applied to
the first of August, could only have originated after the
introduction of the Christian religion in our island, when
the day continuing to be observed as a harvest-thanks-
giving, a loaf of new wheat was the appointed offering at
church. The service was thus called *Hlaf-mass*—Loaf-
mass or *Bread-mass*, gradually changing into Lammas.
Another derivation has been given, namely, from *Lamb-
mass*, "because," says Brand, in his *Popular Antiquities*,
"on that day the tenants who held lands of the Catholic
Church in York, which is dedicated to St. Peter ad
Vincula, were bound by their tenure to bring a live lamb
into the church at high mass;" and again, it has been
suggested that the name arose from a mass to St. Peter
for bespeaking his protection to lambs during the shearing
to keep them from catching cold. But both conjectures
appear to be exceedingly far-fetched. The *Hlaf-mass*,
we submit, affords the most feasible explanation.

In common with the other ancient festivals of the
country, Lammas was long commemorated with sports
and pastimes among the peasantry. Those divertisements,
however, have now fallen into utter desuetude, and,
indeed, it is more than a century since they were practised
in any part of Scotland, although, doubtless, at one time
they were general throughout the kingdom. They seem
to have survived in the Lothians until about the middle
of last century. In 1792 Dr. James Anderson, a popular
writer, and editor of the *Bee*, drew up an account of the
Lothian Lammas, which he contributed to the first
volume of the *Transactions of the Antiquarian Society of*

Scotland, and we shall avail ourselves of this graphic memento of forms and fashions with which the memory of Paganism was kept up for ages after its faith was dead and forgotten.

In an unenclosed corn country, unless the soil is remarkably fertile, a part of the fields must be left in grass for the pasturage of horses, cattle, or sheep; and as all these must be guarded by herds while grazing, it will necessarily happen that in these circumstances a great number of boys and young lads will be employed during the summer months in tending the beasts. About half-a-century ago this was generally the case with the greatest part of the county of Edinburgh. These herds, as is natural for young persons who have much idle time on their hands, devised many kinds of pastime, with which they occasionally diverted themselves, but none was more remarkable than the celebration of the Lammas festival.

All the herds within a certain district, towards the beginning of summer, associated themselves into bands, sometimes to the number of a hundred or more. Each of the communities agreed to build a tower in some conspicuous place, near the centre of their district, which was to serve as the place of their rendezvous on Lammas-day. This tower was usually built of sods, for the most part square, about four feet in diameter at the bottom, and tapering to a point at the top, which was seldom above seven or eight feet from the ground. In building it a hole was left in the centre for admitting a flagstaff, on which they displayed their colours on the great day of the festival. This tower was usually begun to be built about a mouth before Lammas, and was carried up slowly by successive additions from time to time, being seldom entirely completed till a few days before Lammas, though it was always thought that those who completed their's soonest, and kept it standing the longest time before Lammas, behaved in the most gallant manner, and acquired the highest honour by their conduct.

From the moment the foundation of the tower was laid it became an object of care and attention to the whole community, for it was reckoned a disgrace to suffer it to be defaced, so that they resisted with all their power any attempts that should be made to demolish it, either by force or fraud ; and as the honour that was acquired by the demolition of a tower, if effected by those belonging to another, was in proportion to the disgrace of suffering it to be demolished, each party endeavoured to circumvent the other as much as possible, and laid plans to steal upon the other tower unperceived, in the night-time, and level it with the ground. Great was the honour that such a successful exploit conveyed to the undertakers ; and though the tower was easily rebuilt, and soon put in its former state, yet the news was quickly spread by the successful adventurers through the whole district, which filled it with shouts of joy and exultation, while their unfortunate neighbours were covered with shame. To ward off this disgrace, a constant nightly guard was kept at each tower, which was made stronger and stronger as the tower advanced, so that frequent nightly skirmishes ensued at these attacks, but were seldom of much consequence, as the assailants seldom came in force to make an attack in this way, but merely to succeed by surprise ; so soon, therefore, as they saw they were discovered, they made off in the best manner they could.

To give the alarm on these and on other occasions, every person was armed with a "tooting horn," that is, a horn perforated in the small end, through which wind can be forcibly blown from the mouth, so as to occasion a loud sound ; and as every one wished to acquire as great dexterity as possible in the use of this instrument, they practised upon it during the summer while keeping their beasts, and towards Lammas they were so incessantly employed at this business, answering to, and vying with, each other, that the whole country rang continually with the sounds, and it must no doubt have appeared to be a very harsh and unaccountable noise to strangers passing by.

As the great day of Lammas approached, each community chose one from among themselves for their captain ; and they prepared a stand of colours to be ready to be then displayed. For this purpose they usually borrowed a fine table napkin of the largest size, from some of the farmer's wives within the district; and, to ornament it, they also borrowed ribbons from those who would lend them, which they tacked upon the napkin in such fashion as best suited their fancy. Everything being thus prepared, they marched forth early in the morning on Lammas-day, dressed in their best apparel, each armed with a stout cudgel, and repairing to their tower, they displayed their colours in triumph, blowing horns, and making merry in the best manner they could. About nine o'clock they sat down upon the green, and each taking from his pocket bread and cheese, or other provisions, they made a hearty breakfast, drinking pure water from a well, which they always took care should be near the scene of their banquet.

In the meantime, scouts were sent out from every quarter, to bring them notice if any hostile party approached ; for it frequently happened on that day that the herds of one district went to attack those of another district, and to bring them under subjection to them by main force. If news was brought that a hostile party approached, the horns sounded to arms. They were immediately put into the best order they could devise, the stoutest and boldest in front ; and those of inferior prowess behind. Seldom did they await the approach of the enemy, but usually went forth to meet them with a bold countenance, the captain of each party carrying the colours, and leading the van. When they met, they mutually desired each other to lower their colours in sign of subjection ; and if there appeared to be a great dispropor-

tion in the strength of the parties, the weakest usually submitted to this ceremony without much difficulty, thinking their honour was saved by the evident
disproportion of the match. But if they were nearly equal in strength, none
of them would yield, and the rivalry ended in blows, sometimes in bloodshed. A battle of this kind once occurred, in which four were actually killed,
and many wounded. I was once witness to a meeting of this sort, where I
suppose there were more than a hundred on each side, who were so nearly
equal that neither of them would yield. When upon the point of engaging,
a farmer,—a stout, active young man,—who dreaded the consequences, came
galloping up to them, and going between the two parties, with great difficulty, by threats and entreaties, got them to desist till he should speak coolly
to them. He at last got the matter compromised one way or other, so as to
end the strife without blows.

When they had remained at this tower till about midnight, if no opponent appeared, or if they themselves had no intention of making an attack,
they then took down their colours, and marched, with horns sounding, towards the most considerable village in their district, where the lasses, and
all the people, came out to meet them, and partake of their diversions.
Boundaries were immediately appointed, and a proclamation made that all
who intended to compete in the race should appear. A bonnet ornamented
with ribbons was displayed upon a pole, as the prize of the victor; and sometimes five or six started for it, and ran with as great eagerness as if they had
been to gain a kingdom. The prize of the second race was a pair of garters;
and the third, a knife: they then amused themselves for some time with such
rural sports as suited their tastes, and dispersed quietly to their respective
homes before sunset.

When two parties met, and one of them yielded to the other, they marched
together some time in two separate bodies, the subjected body behind the
other, and then they parted good friends, each performing their races at their
own appointed place. Next day, after the ceremony was over, the ribbons
and napkins that formed the colours were carefully returned to their respective owners. The tower was no longer a matter of consequence, and the
country returned to its usual state of tranquility.

The above is a faithful account of this singular ceremony, which was annually repeated in all the country within the distance of six miles west from
Edinburgh, about thirty years ago. How long the custom prevailed, or what
had given rise to it, I am uninformed. The name of Lammas-towers will
remain (some of them having been built of stone) after the celebration of the
festival has ceased. This paper will at least preserve the memory of what
was meant by them. I never could discover the smallest traces of this custom
in Aberdeenshire, though I have there found several towers of stone, very
like the Lammas-towers of this country; but these seem to have been erected
without any appropriated use, but merely to look at. I have known some

of those erected in my time, where I know for certain that no other object
was intended than merely to amuse the persons who erected them.

Thankful are we to Dr. Anderson for thus perpetuating
the memory of the Rustic Sports of Lammas, which, so
far as the races were concerned, might be revived without
any reproach to the " enlightenment of the age."

It would appear that in Ayrshire the end, and not the
beginning, of the harvest season is celebrated by the
youngsters, who kindle fires at the waysides. This custom is called the *Taunel*—a word which Dr. Stratton, of
Devonport, explains to mean the " fire of Baal " or Bel.
"It is strange," he says, "that there is a survival of Pagan
worship among the seven-year-old members of the Ayrshire community." *

* *Celtic Magazine,* Vol. viii., p. 177.

CHAPTER X.

THE HIGHLAND GAMES.

See *Sport*, with *Exercise* and *Health* combin'd,
In happy union.
Mrs. Grant's " Highlanders."

IGHLAND GAMES! What son of the " Land of brown heath and shaggy wood," on hearing these words, will not feel the *perfervidum Scotorum ingenium* stir within his breast, and exclaim :—

" Up wi' the bonnie blue bonnet,
The kilt, and feather, and a'? "

In dealing with the Highland Games, we shall begin with *Camanachd*, or Shinny, which is the same as what the Lowlanders call *Shinty*, and the English *Club-ball ;* but it is not so often played among grown-up Highlanders as it was formerly, being now left much to the youth. About Christmas-tide it was wont to be in high popularity, —the contest generally lying between the men of adjacent parishes ; and pipers were always present, who " skirled " all the time, with might and main, to inspirit the competitors. The prize was a keg of genuine mountain-dew, which, when won, was broached and drunk out on the field by both sides. In some parts of the Highlands the ball is formed of wood, and in others of hard-twisted hair.

Camac has been honoured in song; and dignified in the heroic verse of *The Grampians Desolate:*

> The appointed day is come—th' eventful day,
> When on the snowy field, in firm array,
> Glen meeting glen—(yet not with tempered blades,
> But sapling-oaks cut from the neighbouring glades),
> Engage with ardour keen—in jovial guise,—
> A cask of whisky strong, the victor's prize !
>   'Tis noon, but half the narrow plain is bright,
> The sun just tips the southern hills with light ;
> The mountains gleam that shade the vale below,
> Calm and reflective with encrusted snow.
> Now Dermid, dexterous in manly art,
> And Douglas of the dale, with dauntless heart,
> Lead to the contest fierce their marshalled ranks ;
> To wield their weapons—namely, *shinny-shanks.*

>   .   .   .   .   .   .

> Now front to front the armies in array,
> Await the signal to begin the fray :
> Hark !—'tis the signal !—an ear-piercing smack,
> Which bending echo peals as briskly back ;
> The well-struck ball whirls whizzing thro' the air,
> While each keen combatant, with eager glare,
> Is on th' alert to hit it ere it fall,
> And to th' destined goal urge home the ball :
> Sheer in the centre of the hostile train,
> The orb now rolls along the glittering plain ;
> How brisk the onset !—fearless man meets man
> In kindling ire, of old as clan met clan,
> Aims at the globe, as swells the bickering din,
> Yet hits it not—but hits his neighbour's shin !
> Club rings on sapling-oak,—or shin, or thigh,
> As in the contest champions keenly vie.

>   .   .   .   .

> And still they urge the dubious orb along,
> Till Sol declines the Atlantic waves among ;
> When, with a powerful arm and sapling oak,
> Lo, Douglas to the goal, with giant stroke,
> Home sends the ball !—high peals the joyous " Hail !"
> While Dermid and his heroes gnaw the nail !
> Thus ends the contest—but not so the play,
> Our jovial frolicks close not with the day.

> Behold the victor, with joy-beaming eyes,
> Triumphant marches with the well-won prize,
> And in the hall aloft 'tis placed with care,
> That all anon may drink a liberal share.

An aptitude for athletics seems inherent in the High-lander. His forefathers were " mighty hunters; " but, in strange contrast, they disliked fish and fishing—a dislike attributable perhaps to the fact that fish had some place in the Celtic mythology. Their pastimes were feats of strength and agility, most of which have descended to the present day. Putting the stone, throwing the hammer, and tossing the caber, are amongst the oldest of the High-land games. Tossing the caber is a difficult feat in which few excel. The caber is the branchless trunk of a young tree, which is balanced perpendicularly in both hands, and then suddenly propelled upwards with a jerk, so as to make it describe a somersault before touching the ground. As to the putting stone, we are assured that in former times " it was the custom to have one of these lying at the gate of every chieftain's house, and on the arrival of a stranger, he was asked as a compliment to throw." Another feat was to raise a stone of 200 lb., at least, from the ground, and deposit it upon the top of another, four feet high. The stripling who could accomplish this was thereupon dubbed " a man," and allowed to wear a bonnet : and he attained to the higher dignity of " a pretty man," when he evinced due dexterity in wielding the claymore. Hammer-throwing must have been an every-day recreation at the Highland *smiddies* or forges. The Vulcan of the clachan was an important personage among the primitive society of the glens : and in the *Popular Tales of the West High-lands*, collected by Mr. J. F. Campbell—the familiar stories of the peasantry, recited for generations at the winter hearth and in the summer shealing—the smith occasionally acts a prominent part.   The antiquity of two of the games spoken of appears from "The Story of Conall Gulban." This hero, when on his travels, was asked by "the high-ruler" of a place he had reached, what were the customs of his own people, "and if they tried to do any feats? Conall said that they used to try casting the stone of force *(clach-neart)*, and hurling the hammer.   The high-ruler asked Conall to come in, and he set some to try putting the stone against Conall.   Conall could throw the stone farther than any of them, and they saw that he had no want of strength if there were enough of courage in him." The editor adds in a note to this passage :—"Such games prevailed in ancient Greece long ago, as they still do in the Highlands and Lowlands of Scotland.*   Another feat, once common in the Highlands, and originating obviously among the loungers at a smithy door, was to turn over a thick bar of iron lying on the ground by placing the foot under it.

The sword-dance (called *Gilli-callum* from the accompanying tune), as performed over two drawn swords laid down cross-wise, is held to be modern.   The Germans of Tacitus' time had a sword-dance, which did not escape the observation of the historian.   "One public diversion," he says, "was constantly exhibited at all their meetings ; young men who, by frequent exercise, had attained to great perfection in that pastime, strip themselves, and dance among the points of swords and spears with most wonderful agility, and even with the most elegant and graceful motions.   They do not perform this dance for hire, but for the entertainment of the spectators, esteeming their applause a sufficient reward."   The old Gael had a dance over swords in the Pyrrhic style, and also a

---

* Campbell's *Tales of the West Highlands*, Vol. III., p. 256.

dirk dance ; but both dropt out of fashion, and nobody, it is believed, can now describe what they were. The existing *Gilli-callum*, which arose in their stead, bears, we are told, only a faint resemblance to the original sword-dance of the Highlanders of Scotland.[*]

A Highlander's speed of foot was ever proverbial—the young men being trained to the exercise. The old Highland foot-race, *Geal-ruith*, always included a hurdle leap. Running up the steep breast of a mountain has long been a popular race.

Bagpipe-playing forms an essential feature in the programme of a Highland competition :—the bagpipe being now regarded as the Scottish Gael's distinctive musical instrument, though the harp once ranked higher with his ancestors. The harp has vanished from the Highlands ; yet it was coeval, at least, with the bagpipe, and more honoured among the ancient Celts. " The harp," says a competent judge, " is the true instrument of Gaelic song, which we had of old in common with our brethren the Gael of Ireland, among whom the great bagpipe was never known."[†] " The Bards of the Celts," according to Ammianus Marcellinus, a writer of the fourth century, " celebrated the actions of illustrious men in heroic poems, which they sung to the sweet sounds of the lyre." At the feast of shells, " in the days of song," Fingal " heard the music of harps, the tales of other times." And the soul of Ossian, in his age, and solitude, and darkness, yearned to his harp as the last solace : " Bends there not a tree from Mora with its branches bare ? It bends, son of Alpin, in the rustling blast. My harp hangs on a blasted branch. The sound of its strings is mournful.

---

[*] Logan's *Scottish Gael*, Vol. II., pp. 302, 307.
[†] *The Grampians Desolate.* Notes, p. 268.

Does the wind touch thee, O harp, or is it some passing ghost ? It is the hand of Malvina ! Bring me the harp, son of Alpin. Another song shall arise. My soul shall depart in the sound. My fathers shall hear it in their airy hall. Their dim faces shall hang, with joy, from their clouds ; and their hands receive their son." To the warrior, the harp was the voice of fame : its music was the most grateful to the people ; the child in its cradle was soothed and charmed by the soft melody. Trathal's spouse, in the poem, "had remained at home. Two children rose with their fair locks about her knees. They bend their ears above the harp as she touched, with her white hand, the trembling strings. She stops. They take the harp themselves, but cannot find the sound they admired. 'Why,' they said, 'does it not answer us ? Show us the string where dwells the song.' She bids them search for it till she returns. Their little fingers wander among the wires." For centuries, the accomplishment of singing to the harp was deemed an indispensable part of the education of the upper grade of Highland society, and at festivals the harp was handed round that each of the company might sing to it.* Mary Queen of Scots played on the harp. During her excursion to Athole, in 1564, she is said to have gifted a harp, ornamented with jewels, to an ancestress of the Robertsons of Lude, who bore the palm at a competition of harp-players which took place in the royal presence. This precious relic of the beautiful, but ill-starred Queen, was carefully preserved by that family, along with a still more ancient harp which had come to them in 1460 through marriage with an Argyleshire lady. When the blind bard, Rory Dall, or Roderick Morison, one of the last of the trained

---

* Gunn's *Harp in the Highlands*, p. 55.

and professional Highland harpers, visited Lude in company with the Marquis of Huntly, about the year 1650, the Queen's harp was put into his hands, and he composed a *port* or air in honour of the occasion, which was called *Suipar Chiurn na Leod*, or The Supper of Lude. In the time of the rebellion of 1745 this instrument was despoiled of its precious stones, either by the persons to whose care it had been confided for concealment, or, as they asserted, by the Duke of Cumberland's soldiers. It was recently in the possession of the Stewarts of Dalguise ; and the other old harp seems to have been ultimately deposited with the Highland Society of Scotland.

The last appearance of the Highland harp on the field of battle was at Glenlivat, 3rd October, 1594, when the Earl of Argyll, as the royal lieutenant, encountered the rebel Roman Catholic lords, Huntly and Errol. To encourage the clansmen, of whom his army was mainly composed, Argyll brought his harper with him, and also a sorceress, who predicted that, on the following Friday, his harp should sound in Buchan and his pibroch in Strathbogie—the provinces of his enemies. But the battle took place on Thursday, the royal troops were routed, and the Pytheness herself perished in the slaughter. A writer of the end of the sixteenth century states that the Highlanders "delight much in musick, but chiefly in harpes," which "they take great pleasure to deck with silver and precious stones ; and the poore ones that cannot attain heereunto deck them with cristall." * The harp-keys or *wrests* were also richly adorned : one, which had belonged to Rory Dall, and was kept at Armidale in 1772, when Dr. Johnson and Boswell were in

---

* "Description of Scotland," appended to Monipennie's *Abridgement of the Scots Chronicles.*

the Hebrides, was "finely ornamented with silver and gold, and a precious stone, and valued at more than eighty guineas." Every chieftain kept his hereditary bard, who celebrated the honour and renown of the sept ; but this fashion, together with the use of the harp, gradually declined—that instrument being apparently superseded by the violin, which became fashionable in the seventeenth century ; though, we must remember that the violin's precursor, the viol or *cruit*, was known in the north perhaps as early as the harp itself. The harp was finally discontinued in the Scottish Highlands about 1734, leaving the bagpipe master of the field.

The high antiquity of the Highland bagpipe is indisputable ; and the pipe-music is endeared to the people by "the stirring memory of a thousand years." Many of the airs, though seeming rude to a polished ear, are peculiarly plaintive, and exert an influence over the unsophisticated feelings of a Celt similar to that of the *Ranz de Vaches* on a Swiss mountaineer. How often have the salt tears hailed down the cheeks of the expatriated Gael when "Lochaber no more" brought back to his mind's eye the never-to-be-forgotten mountains and vales, the rolling rivers and the dashing cataracts, the rocks of the eagles, and the forests of the deer! Each clan had its own *Piobrachd*—a war tune, "savage and shrill," which incited to the fray or celebrated a victory : and each clan had likewise its own *Cum-hadh* or lament for the dead. One piece of pipe-music is said to date from 1314, and was played before the Clan Donnachy or Robertsons of Athole when they marched to Bannockburn. It is named *Theachd Clann Donnachaidh*—The Coming of the Robertsons. But the most ancient tune known is *Comha Somhairle*—Somerled's Lament—which was composed on the assassination of that leader at Renfrew, in his own camp, in 1164. "The bagpipe is sacred to Scotland, and speaks a language which Scotsmen only feel. There is not a battle that is honourable to Britain in which its war-blast has not sounded. When every other instrument has been hushed by the confusion and carnage of the scene, it has been borne into the thick of the battle, and, far in the advance, its bleeding but devoted bearer, sinking on the earth, has sounded at once encouragement to his country-men and his own coronach." * Highland music, more-over, is widely diversified, giving expression to all the varied moods. Look at the festive gatherings where

> Native music wakes in sprightly strains,
> Which gay according motion best explains :
> Fastidious Elegance, in scornful guise,
> Perhaps the unpolished measure may despise ;
> But here, where infant lips in tuneful lays,
> And Melody her untaught charms displays ;
> The dancers bound with wild peculiar grace,
> And Sound thro' all its raptur'd mazes trace ;
> Nor awkward step, nor rude ungainly mien,
> Through all the glad assemblage can be seen.

What can be more spirit-stirring and mirth-inspiring than the "strathspeys and reels," which "put life and mettle in the heels" of a population exceedingly fond of saltatory diversion ?

It is on such an occasion as a Gathering for competition in Highland games, that Donald Macdonald is seen in all his pride and glory. He then struts forth in holiday spirits as well as in holiday attire, resolved to do his utmost to impress favourably the minds of those Sassenach strangers, who throng northwards in autumn with the same regularity as the Highland reapers used to descend in bands to the golden-waving plains of the Lowlands.

---

* M'Donald's *Ancient Martial Music of Caledonia.*

" Idstone," an English sporting writer, who was present, at a meeting among the Grampians, about a dozen of years since, paid a generous compliment (in the columns of *The Field*) to the Highland character :—

On two sides ran a rapid winding hill-stream ; on the third side was a *big mountain*—according to my Lowland views ; and on the fourth were the marquees, the refreshment-stalls and the judges' tent. The mountain-side was occupied by a motley assemblage of gay colours—kilts, pipers, and competitors. In the circle where the games were to take place a chosen circle chatted together beneath a large flag, bearing an inscription which " no fellow could understand." The benches for the ladies were gradually filling, for it was just twelve o'clock, and the assistants were fast bringing in the various implements necessary for the games.

One could not help contrasting this scene with English ideas of athleticism as they *did* exist—the "stakes," the "referee," the "cinder-path," the "beer," the impudent landlord and his gate-money, the long pipes and pot-stained tables of the past, the sham Indian runners, the professional ped.," or (save the mark !) the pigeons, and the professional pigeon shots wrangling over guns and charges, sweepstakes and distances.

The scenery, the picturesque effective northern garb, and the national character of the gathering, had much to do with the general effect of the meeting ; and the superior education of the Scotch peasant decidedly influenced the proceedings. You heard no coarse language—least of all profane oaths—from the competitors. There was no "dog trial" wrangling as to the awards. The defeated piper appeared equally pleased when he was adjudged second or third rate as a player of reels ; the marksmen at the rifle-butts were polite and self-possessed whether they lost or won.

Long may Donald retain the simple, decorous, manly manners, and the independent self-respect, which merit such encomiums !

CHAPTER XI.

CURLING.

When chittering birds, on flicht'ring wing,
    About the barn doors mingle,
And biting frost, and cranreuch cauld,
    Drive coofs around the ingle;
Then to the loch the curlers hie,
    Their hearts as light's a feather,
And mark the tee wi' mirth and glee,
    In cauld, cauld frosty weather.

Rev. James Muir.

AMONG the popular sports and pastimes of the "Land of Cakes," there is one which is vaunted as being exclusively national—"Scotland's ain game o' Curling." Well-merited are the ardent panegyrics which have been lavished upon it! What winter recreation can rival the Bonspiel? The "keen, keen curler" exults when Boreas and John Frost are in their bitterest moods, muffling Mother Earth in her winding-sheet and congealing the waters to the consistency of stone. Look at the thronged and resounding rink on a clear, hard, nipping day, when

The ice is here, the ice is there,
    The ice is all around:

and your heart will warm and leap in unison with the geniality and good fellowship pervading the busy assemblage! As admirably conducive to the promotion of genuine fraternity between all classes of men, curling must be pronounced unequalled among games.

> For on the water's face are met,
>   Wi' mony a merry joke man,
> The tenant and his jolly laird,
>   The pastor and his flock, man.

Need we strive to depict the deepening contest that animates the snowy scene? This has been done to our hand by the amiable poet of the Sabbath, in his *British Georgics:*

> Now rival parishes, and shrievedoms, keep,
> On upland lochs, the long-expected tryst
> To play their yearly bonspiel. Aged men,
> Smit with the eagerness of youth, are there,
> While love of conquest lights their beamless eyes,
> New-nerves their arms, and makes them young once more.
>   The sides when ranged, the distance meted out,
> And duly traced the tees, some younger hand
> Begins, with throbbing heart, and far o'ershoots,
> Or sideward leaves, the mark : in vain he bends
> His waist, and winds his hand, as if it still
> Retained the power to guide the devious stone,
> Which, onward hurling, makes the circling group
> Quick start aside, to shun its reckless force.
> But more and still more skilful arms succeed,
> And near and nearer still around the tee
> This side, now that, approaches ; till at last,
> Two seeming equidistant, straws or twigs
> Decide as umpires 'tween contending coits.
>   Keen, keener still, as life itself were staked,
> Kindles the friendly strife : one points the line
> To him who, poising, aims and aims again ;
> Another runs and sweeps where nothing lies.
> Success alternately, from side to side,
> Changes ; and quick the hours un-noted fly,
> Till light begins to fail, and deep below,

The player, as he stoops to lift his coit,
Sees, half-incredulous, the rising moon,
But now the final, the decisive spell,
Begins ; near and more near the sounding stones,
Some winding in, some bearing straight along,
Crowd jostling all around the mark, while one,
Just slightly touching, victory depends
Upon the final aim : long swings the stone,
Then with full force, careering furious on,
Rattling it strikes aside both friend and foe,
Maintains its course, and takes the victor's place.
The social meal succeeds, and social glass ;
In words the fight renewed is fought again,
While festive mirth forgets the winged hours.

No trace of curling can be found among the out-door amusements of the English in former days. On the other hand, the claim that it is indigenous to Scotland—seems at the best somewhat problematical. The scanty and fragmentary history of curling in Scotland points to the theory that the "roaring play" was an importation from the Low Countries. Some of the chief technical terms of the game appear to owe their derivation to the Dutch or German. *Curl* may have come from the German word *Kurzweil*—a game, and *Curling* from *Kurzweillen*—to play for amusement. The old name for curling in some parts of Scotland was *Kuting* or *Cooting*, and the stones were called *Cooting* or *Coiting*-stones—evidently from the Teutonic *Kluyten*—to play with round pieces of ice, in the manner of quoits, on a sheet of ice ; or, the denomination may have come from the Dutch *coete*—a quoit ; as if, indeed, the game of quoits, and not that of bowls, originated curling. The word *Bonspiel*, as understood in Scotland, signifies a match at any game—curling, golf, football, archery, etc., and it has even been applied in some quarters to a prize-fight ! Perhaps it comes from the French *bon* and the German *speilen ;* but the more likely derivation is from the Belgic *bonne*, a village or district, and *spel*, play—thus expressing a friendly competition between people of different townships or parishes. *Tee* is the winning point: Icelandic *tia*, to point out; and *witter* is another name for the tee: Suio-Gothic *wittra*, to point out. *Wick*—Suio-Gothic *wik*, a corner; and only a corner of the stone is hit in the operation of what is called wicking. *Skip*—a director of the play: Suio-Gothic, *skeppare;* whence skipper of a ship. *Hack*, or *hatch*, a cut on the ice, to save the foot of the player from slipping when delivering the stone: Icelandic *hiacka*, or Suio-Gothic *hack*, a crack. From which etymological coincidences, taken in conjunction with the period when curling is first mentioned as being played in Scotland, the inference has been drawn that the game was introduced by the numerous companies of Flemings who emigrated from Flanders to Scotland about the end of the fifteenth and beginning of the sixteenth centuries.

Now, let any stickler for the indigenousness of Curling in Scotland explain how it comes to pass that the earliest notices of the game crop up only in the seventeenth century. Look at the sports and pastimes which our James IV. patronized, as set out in full detail in the Lord High Treasurer's Accounts. Is Curling, or the remotest trace of it, there? Does Dunbar mention it? Does Sir David Lyndsay, or any other poet of the sixteenth century? At the same time, we do not forget that the game seemed unknown in Germany and the Low Countries until of late years, and no mention of its former existence there has been discovered in any record. But the signification of *kluyten* shows that the Germans had once a game similar to curling—namely, throwing or sliding lumps of ice upon the frozen surface of water, apparently in imitation of the game of quoits. Besides, the utter extinction of curling on the Continent is not so very improbable a supposition, when we know that, although curling was introduced into Ireland by the Scottish colonists of the time of James I. of England, it soon fell into oblivion there, and has only been recently revived. Unquestionably the Teutonic tongue still lingers in the game, and no conjecture has the plausibility of that which assigns the origin of curling to the people whose language is connected with it.

Until within the early part of the present century, curling was neither practised nor even known *universally* in Scotland. Some provinces knew nothing about it. Among the ancient sports of the Highland population, it had no place. It was entirely a Lowland pastime. The earliest notices of curling in Scotland appear in the Perth poet, Henry Adamson's *Muses Threnodie*, published in 1638, and reprinted in 1774. The author makes his aged friend, Mr. George Ruthven, a Perth physician and antiquary, speak thus—

> And ye my *loadstones* of *Lednochian lakes*,
> Collected from the loughs, where watery snakes
> Do much abound, take unto you a part,
> And mourn for *Gall*, who lov'd you with his heart.
> In this sad dump and melancholic mood,
> The *burdown* ye must bear, not on the flood
> Or frozen watery plains, but let your tuning
> Come help me for to weep by mournful cruning.

The "loadstones" were curling stones brought from Lednoch or Lynedoch (the scene of Bessy Bell and Mary Gray's story) on the banks of the Almond ; and a note in the edition of 1774 explains that "the gentlemen of Perth, fond of this athletic winter-diversion on the frozen river, sent and brought from Lednoch their curling stones." Farther, " The Inventory of the Gabions (curiosities, etc.), in Mr. George Ruthven's Closet or Cabinet," which prefaces the poem, enumerates—

> His alley bowls, his *curling-stones*,
> The sacred games to celebrate,
> Which to the gods are consecrate.*

In the same year which saw Adamson's work "touch the press" and "come to light," the Bishop of Orkney, who, along with the rest of the Scottish Prelates, suffered deposition by the General Assembly of the Kirk which met at Glasgow, was stigmatized by his Covenanting enemies as a "Curler on the Lord's Day."

Other notices of the game in the subsequent portion of the century are equally meagre and incidental.

In Bishop Gibson's edition of Camden's *Britannia*, 1695, a reference to curling is added in connection with the isle of Copinsha, one of the Orkneys, "in which," it is said, "and in several other places of this country, are to be found in great plenty excellent stones for the game called Curling."

Lord Fountainhall, in his *Decisions*, under date 1684, states :—" A party of the forces having been sent out to apprehend Sir William Scott of Harden, younger, one William Scott in Langhope, getting notice of their coming, went and acquainted Harden with it as he was playing at the Curling with Riddel of Haining and others."

Passing to the next century, we hear of another clergyman charged with the crime of curling out of season. A letter from Mr. Charles Cokburne, son of the Lord Justice-Clerk of Scotland, addressed to the Duke of Montrose, and dated at Edinburgh, 2nd June, 1715, intimates the trial at Perth of an Episcopal clergyman, named Mr. Guthrie, who intruded into a church, not praying for King George, nor keeping the Thanksgiving for his

---

* *The Muses Threnodie* (1774), Vol. I., pp. 5, 18.

Majesty's accession, but "going to the curling that day," and drinking the Pretender's health on his birthday.* In 1715, likewise, Dr. Alexander Pennecuik of Newhall gave his poems to the world, and in one of his effusions makes a very complimentary allusion to curling, shewing that the game was popular in his day and neighbourhood :—

> To curl on the ice does greatly please,
> Being a manly Scottish exercise ;
> It clears the brains, stirs up the native heat,
> And gives a gallant appetite for meat.

While the rebellion of 1745 was at its height, a curling match took place at Blairgowrie, and the usual " beef and greens " having been provided, a party of Prince Charlie's Highlanders made a foray on the tempting dinner, and effectually disposed of it, to the great disappointment and dismay of the hungry competitors. An anecdote is also related of the Rev. Mr. Lyon, who was minister of Blairgowrie parish from 1723 to 1768. The worthy incumbent was so fond of curling that he continued to pursue it, with unabated ardour, even after old age had left him scarce strength enough to send a stone beyond the hog-score ; and on one occasion, having over-exerted himself in the act of delivering his stone, he lost his balance and fell on his back. Some of the bystanders hastened to his assistance ; and, in the meantime, one of the party placed the stone he had just thrown off on the centre of the tee. While still on his back the minister eagerly inquired where his stone was, and being informed that it was on the tee, exclaimed, "Oh, then, I'm no a bit waur !" †

Mr. Pennant first visited Scotland in 1769, crossing the Border at Berwick ; but his volume, describing the tour,

---

* *Third Report on Historical Manuscripts*, p. 373.

† *Annual of the Grand Caledonian Curling Club for 1842.*

has no mention of curling, for evidently, throughout his peregrinations, he had never heard of the game. In the summer of 1772 he came back, this time crossing by the west marches, and as soon as he got within the country of "Blinkin' Bess o' Annandale" and "Maggy by the banks o' Nith," he became aware of what recreation they pursued in winter. "Of the sports of these parts," he says, "that of *curling* is a favourite, and one unknown in England : it is an amusement of the winter and played on the ice, by sliding from one mark to another great stones of forty to seventy pounds weight, of a hemispherical form, with an iron or wooden handle at top. The object of the player is to lay his stone as near to the mark as possible to guard that of his partner, which had been well laid before, or to strike off that of his antagonist." * A good and clear description of the game by a Southron.

Recurring to the question of the origin and antiquity of the game in Scotland, it must be noted that no old curling-stones are extant of unquestioned dates earlier than the seventeenth century at the farthest. The author of the *Memorabilia Curliana Mabenensia*, himself an enthusiastic curler, and to whose book we owe many obligations, has observed—"Another circumstance leads to the supposition that the origin of the game, in this country at least, is not very remote,—the specimens that still remain of the unhandled, unpolished blocks which were used by the curlers of, comparatively, even modern times. The improvements since adopted are so obvious that they must have suggested themselves long before the time when they actually were made, had the practice of the game been very ancient. Though no evidence exists

---

* *A Tour in Scotland, and Voyage to the Hebrides, 1772.* Chester, 1774 ; p. 81.

to show that curling is now practised, or that it ever was practised, on the Continent, further than what arises from the etymology of the art, as above noticed, yet we have evidence that something very like it was at one time in operation there. Kilian, in his dictionary, renders the Teutonic *kluyten kallyuten*—ludere massis sive globis glaciatis, certare discis in æquore glaciato. Whatever those round masses of ice were, they seem to have been employed in a game on the ice after the manner of quoits. Indeed, it is highly probable that the game we now call curling was nothing else than the game of quoits practised upon the ice. The old stones which yet remain, both from size and shape, favour the conjecture, having only a niche for the finger and thumb, as if they had been intended to be thrown." [*] Some old stones, however, have been found both handled and dated. An unhammered curling - stone was found in an old curling pond near Dunblane, bearing the date 1551 ; but the age of the inscription has been much doubted. In the dry summer of 1826, an old stone was recovered from the bottom of the Shiels Loch, near Roslin, which had been dried up by the great drought, and which the Roslin people had used time out of mind for curling. The stone was found embedded in the mud, and was about to be consigned to the walls of the new chapel of Roslin, which were then being erected, when the mason, by the merest accident, discovered that the " channel stane" bore the date 1613. The stone was a grey whin, $5\frac{1}{2}$ inches thick, of triangular form, and quite rough as it came out of the bed of the river ; while the handle had been iron, which was entirely corroded away, but the lead remained. The triangular shape of this stone re-

---

[*] *Memorabilia Curliana Mabenensia.* Dumfries : 1830, p. 10.

sembles that of the "goose" of other days, which was generally employed as the "prentice stone" given to young players to try their hands on. The "goose" served both as a "leader" and "wheeler": in the first capacity it was a dangerous shot when well played, leading many a stone directed against it a wild-goose chase, by fairly turning round like a Jim Crow, as it never moved from the spot except when hit exactly in the centre. In the month of December, 1830, while the foundation of the old House of Loig, in Strathallan, was being dug out, a curling-stone of peculiar shape was discovered. It was of an oblong form, and had been neatly finished with the hammer, and bore the date 1611. One of the same date was got at Torphichen. About half-a-dozen old curling stones were unearthed in digging a drain to the east of Watson's Hospital, near Edinburgh. They were all roughly made, but had handles, though no dates. They were allowed to lie about the field for a fortnight, till they were all broken to pieces (perhaps for the sake of the iron of the handles), save one, a fair sample of the rest. It was a semi-spheroidical block of coarse-grained whinstone, weighing 65 lb., —about six inches high,—and with an iron handle of the common kind fixed in the usual place. Not long ago, on the draining of a small loch at Ardoch, a considerable number of old curling stones were found at the bottom : all had handles, and one was marked 1700, with the letters M. W. H. Some other stones have been found in various quarters, but need not be particularized.

The Grand (now Royal) Caledonian Curling Club was instituted in 1838, the year of the hard winter. The jubilee of the Club was celebrated by a dinner in the Waterloo Hotel, Edinburgh, on the 28th November, 1888, presided over by the Marquis of Breadalbane. In alluding to the institution of the Club, the noble chairman said :—

"Nothing was done in the way of forming a club until an anonymous advertisement appeared in the *North British Advertiser* in May, 1838. Only about a dozen curlers attended the meeting thus called, which was held in the very house in which they were now dining. It was obvious, from the smallness of the attendance, that no business could be done, and the meeting was adjourned. A second advertisement was inserted, calling a meeting of curlers on the 25th July, 1838, and stating that Mr. John Tierney would occupy the chair. He did occupy the chair, deputations appeared from various clubs, and at that meeting the Grand Caledonian Curling Club sprang into existence." We have chosen thus to mark the institution of the Grand Club, rather than to occupy space unnecessarily by referring to the various local clubs which were previously in existence.

CHAPTER XII.

MISCELLANEOUS.

Healthful sports that graced the peaceful scene.
Goldsmith's " Deserted Village."

I.—BOWLS.

THE game of *Bowls* has been traced in England back to the thirteenth century, and there it had the honour of being at last denounced by the legislature as prejudicial to archery. Bluff King Hal played at the bowls, and made bowling-alleys at White-hall, but had no scruple in preventing other people from playing when the archers complained. The Act which passed in his time against various pastimes, including bowls, remained on the Statute Book till 1845, when it was repealed.

In Scotland the game was popular for ages, and never proscribed. Royalty patronized it. Bowling-greens became adjuncts of Scottish mansion-houses and castles. The old ballad of "The Bonnie House o' Airly" relates how the Lady Margaret's dowry or treasure was found by the Marquis of Argyll's men, hidden about the bowling-green.

> They sought it up, they sought it down,
>   They sought it late and early,
> And found it in the bonnie balm-tree
>   That shines on the bowling-green o' Airly.

But a weird tradition of the Second Sight, noted in Wodrow's *Analecta*, tells how Argyll afterwards got a fore-warning of his fate under the axe of the "Scottish Maiden," while he was engaged in a game of bowls with some gentlemen of his clan. "One of the players, when the Marquis stooped down to lift the bullet (bowl), fell pale, and said to them about him, 'Bless me! what is that I see? My Lord with the head off, and all his shoulders full of blood.'"

Dr. Thomas Somerville of Jedburgh, in his retrospect of the social state of Scotland during the earlier period of his lifetime, beginning with 1741, says: "Many of our national games, as handball, football, golf and curling, though not discontinued, are less generally practised than when I was a young man. Bowls were then a common amusement. Every country town was provided with a public bowling-green for the diversion of the inhabitants in the summer evenings. All classes were represented among the players, and it was usual for players of different ranks to take part in the same game. A bowling-green usually formed part of the *policy* or pleasure grounds of country houses. At these private bowling-greens ladies also shared in the amusement, thus rendering it greatly more attractive." *

Much interesting matter might be adduced respecting the public Bowling Greens of the Scottish cities and towns, beginning with the capital, many of whose douce folk were often seen (by Allan Ramsay)

> Wysing a-jee
> The byas bowls on Tamson's green.

But our space is diminishing fast, and we shall content

---

* *My Own Life and Times*, p. 345.

ourselves with a few curious notices of the management of the old Bowling Green at Cowan's Hospital, in Stirling.

The Town Council of Stirling, with the minister of the First Charge, are the patrons or managers of Cowan's Hospital, one of the charitable institutions of the town. On 16th January, 1738, "the patrons considering a petition given in by several of the merchants, trades, and other inhabitants, showing the badness of the Bowling Green, and craving the same might be laid with salt faill, they therefore appoint the masters" of the hospital "to cause William Dawson, gardener, and keeper of the said Green, to lay the same with salt faill as soon as possible, the expense thereof not exceeding the sum of £10 sterling." In March, next year, the expense of the improvements was found to be £138 4s. Scots, or £11 16s. 8d. Sterling; and the patrons ordered "the bowl meal (mail, or charge) to be augmented to one shilling Scots (a penny, Sterling) from each person playing." On March 22, 1740, "the patrons appoint the master to provide half-a-dozen pair of byass bowls to the Bowling Green, and to cause make a sufficient lodge for the bowls in a proper part of the garden." The bowls seem to have served for fourteen years, as on 6th April, 1754, "the patrons appoint the master to provide six pair of new bowls and an odd one for the use of the Hospital Bowling Green, a great many of those already there being almost useless." Again, on 5th February, 1763, eight pairs of good byass bowls and two jacks were ordered to be purchased for the use of the Green. The price was £3 6s. 10d. Sterling, paid to Robert Home, merchant in Edinburgh.

Improvements in the management of the Green became imperatively necessary in 1777. On 16th May, that year,

" the managers considering that of late great complaints
have been made to them that the Hospital Green, flower
garden, and back walk are not kept in the same good
order and condition which they used to be in : that people
are allowed without distinction not only to make a
thoroughfare of the garden, but also to use the Bowling
Green contrary to the original intention thereof; they
therefore authorise the Hospital master to give orders to
the keeper of the said Green with regard to the proper
management and regulation thereof, so as that improper
persons may be prevented from taking up the Green ;
and appoint the said keeper to obey the orders that may
be given him from time to time by the Hospital master
thereanent, at his peril; and authorize the Hospital
master to cause build a small brick house for holding the
bowls, in such convenient situation as may be pointed out
by the managers."   Still there was dissatisfaction, and on
5th July, 1779, the magistrates framed a set of Regula-
tions for the Keeper of the Hospital Green, etc., the following being the principal :—" Not to suffer boys and
others to make a common thoroughfare of the garden and
terraces, but to keep the garden doors lockt, and to give
attendance to let decent people, as well strangers as
town's folk, pass through them.   To await regularly on
the Bowling Green, to allow none but decent people to
play at bowls, and no children or servant-maids, etc., to
walk on the Green."

As a quiet and healthful recreation, particularly for
sedentary persons and those who cannot join in sports
requiring a great exertion of physical strength, the game
of bowls, we are glad to observe, has of late years been
extending in many quarters.

II.—RIDING AT THE RING, AND RUNNING AT THE GLOVE.

Riding or Tilting at the Ring, and *Running at the Glove*, were favourite pastimes of the days of chivalry. We read in the old Scottish ballad :

> He was a braw gallant,
>   And he rid at the ring ;
> And the bonnie Earl of Murray,
>   Oh ! he might ha'e been a king.
>
> He was a braw gallant,
>   And he play'd at the ba' ;
> And the bonnie Earl of Murray
>   Was the flower amang them a'.
>
> He was a braw gallant,
>   And he play'd at the gluve ;
> And the bonnie Earl of Murray,
>   Oh ! he was the Queen's luve.

Tilting at the Ring consisted in mounted competitors galloping singly, spear in hand, towards a ring which was suspended by a spring in a sheath affixed to a transverse beam on a pole, at a slight elevation above their heads, and endeavouring to bring off the ring on the point of the spear—three courses in succession being allowed each competitor to accomplish the feat.

James VI., in his *Basilikon*, bids his son " specially use such games on horseback, as may teach you to handle your arms thereon ; such as the tilt, *the ring*, and low-riding for handling of your sword."

Up to about the end of last century, Tilting at the Ring was a favourite sport of the different Societies of Scottish Chapmen, at their annual gatherings for the election of office-bearers. It is said that a right to engage in this game was granted by James I. to the Chapmen of Stirling ; and " a tilting lance used at the Chapmen's Sports during the reign of James V., is preserved in the armoury of Stirling Castle."* The Minutes of the Guildry of Stirling show that in 1707 the Incorporation resolved to "cause make ane gold ring to be ridden for at the Ring," on the occasion of a local fair, " by the Dean of Guild, Treasurer, and twelve Guild brethren, whom the Dean of Guild and Magistrates shall name, and any strangers who shall think fit to ride thereat ; and recommends to the Dean of Guild and Treasurer to put what motto shall be most proper on the said ring." Nearly fifty years afterwards, in 1751, the Guildry ordered the ring, or an equivalent of 20s., to be given to the Chapmen, "and yearly thereafter during the Guildry's pleasure." This grant continued to be given till 1768, when the Guildry " instead of paying the Chapman 20s. sterling for a Ring for their Race, allow them to collect the Wax-meall (dues on Bees-wax) payable by the several Chapmen, etc., for having the benefit of the Market, and to apply the same for buying a Ring." Next year, however, the Guildry ordered the Treasurer to pay the Chapmen whatever was deficient of 20s. in the amount of the wax-duty. This arrangement lasted till 1778, when the Guildry reverted to the original " complement of 20s. for a Ring to the Chapmen," which appears in the Minutes up till 1784. The Chapmen themselves, in 1795, resolved to have a Horse Race instead of Ring-riding, and directed " an application for getting from the Guildry the 20s. which was formerly given for a Ring-race to be applied towards a Horse Race." But in 1800 the Stirling Chapmen changed themselves into a mere Friendly Society, having nothing more to do with Ring or Horse races.

---

* Dr. Rogers' *Scotland, Social and Domestic*, p. 184.

In our own day, Tilting at the Ring has held place among popular games in some districts of Scotland, such as in the sports of the town of Lanark's festival called "Lanimer Day." A Lanarkshire gentleman, writing to a London paper in June 1874, states that every year at Carnwath, on the estate of the Lockharts of Lee (the ancient house possessing the *Lee Penny*), a foot-race is run for "a pair of red hose" given by the Lee family, and the legend is that they hold their lands under a Charter which enjoins this being done annually. At this meeting, Tilting at the Ring has been carried on for a very lengthened period, the prize being a gold ring, given by the Lady Lockhart of the day. A competition of the same kind took place, with stiff hurdles on both sides of the transverse beam and ring within the Hamilton Palace policy grounds. The public were admitted, and large crowds attended. In 1873 a public competition was held at Hamilton, several of the officers of the 1st Royal Dragoons, quartered at Hamilton, competing along with a large number of other gentlemen. The writer adds—"As to private competitions among friends, I have witnessed hundreds of them; and, while tilting on level ground without hurdles is sometimes practised, it is considered poor fun without a 'lep' on each side, the hurdles being generally 3 ft. 3 in. to 3 ft. 6 in. high, at fifteen yards distance from the transverse beam on each side, and the ring has to be taken off and carried on the lance over the second hurdle." Another correspondent holds that this pastime "far excels in manly skill and horsemanship the now famous game of Polo."

When a glove was substituted for the ring, the sport was called *Running at the Glove*. The substitution was in this way: the glove, instead of being suspended in the air, was laid on the ground, and the art of the sport was for a cavalier riding past at the gallop to pick it up on the point of his lance.

Dr. Magnus and Roger Ratcliffe, the English envoys at the Scottish Court during the minority of James V., wrote to Cardinal Wolsey on 15th November, 1524, when James was but a boy of thirteen: "The Queen's said grace hath had us furth to solace with the King's grace here, at Leith and in the fields, and to see his said grace stir his horses, and *run with a spear*, amongst other his lords and servants, *at a glove*." *

Robert Armin, in his *Nest of Ninnies*, 1608 (reprinted by the Shakespeare Society in 1842), has a jocular story about Jemmy Camber, a royal fool, riding at the glove, on a mule, in "an even plain grass meadow" betwixt Edinburgh and Leith.

In the account of expenses of the festivities on the marriage of Francis, Earl of Buccleugh, and Lady Margaret Leslie, in July and October, 1646 (among the Rothes Papers), is an entry: "For 3 dozen of spears for running at the glove, £24." †

III.—CAITCH-BALL.

Caitch-ball (a variety of tennis) is a very old Scottish game, consisting in the striking of a leather-covered ball against a high wall, with the hand, and after it rebounds, falls to the ground, and rises, striking it back again. That it was played with the hand is shown in a poetical bundle of impossibilities, called "Woman's Truth," preserved in the Bannatyne MS.:

---

* Tytler's *History of Scotland* (1864), Vol. II., p. 332, note.
† *Fourth Report on Historical MSS.*, p. 509.

> Ane handless man I saw but dreid
> In caichpule fast playing.*

The "caichpule" was the court or place in which the game was played.

The game frequently appears in the Lord High Treasurer's Accounts in the time of James IV. The following sums were paid to the King, "to play at the cach," while he was in Stirling: 1496, May, £6 10s., and June, £2 14s.; 1497, September, £2 14s.; 1498, April, £5, and May, £18. James VI., in his *Basilikon*, recommends "playing at the *caitch* or tennis."

IV.—THE KILES.

The *Kiles* were what are now called Skittles or Nine-pins. Strutt says: "Kayles, written also *cayles* and *keiles*, derived from the French word *quilles*, was played with pins, and no doubt gave origin to the modern game of nine-pins; though primitively the kayle-pins do not appear to have been confined to any certain number;" and he gives instances of six and eight pins being used. "The arrangement of the kayle-pins differs greatly from that of the nine-pins, the latter being placed upon a square frame in three rows, and the former in one row only." There was a variety of the game called club-kayles, in which a stick was thrown at them.†

James IV. sometimes played at the Kiles. After the Reformation, the game was another cause of Sabbath desecration. In the minutes of the Kirk-Session of Perth, under date of 6th October, 1589, we read that "as at the playing of the Kylles in the North and South Inches, the

---

* *A Book of Scottish Pasquils*, p. 4.
† *Sports and Pastimes*, p. 270.

Sabbath is broken and God's holy name profaned," the Session "ordains the bailies to break them, and note their names that play at them, and give them in to the Assembly ilk Monday, that they may be punished."

V.—CRICKET.

Cricket is of English origin, and was only introduced at a comparatively recent period into Scotland, where it has become thoroughly naturalized. In its origin, it was probably an offshoot from the old pastime of club-ball, which was played in England as early as in the thirteenth or fourteenth centuries; but when cricket first became a distinct game has not been decided. The scholars of the Free School at Guildford played cricket in the reign of Queen Elizabeth—this being the earliest mention of the game by its modern name, though it seems to have existed long before under another name.

> See where the school-boy, once again dismiss'd,
> Feels all the bliss of liberty, and drives
> The speedy hour away at the brisk games
> Of social cricket. It delights me much
> To see him run, and hear the cheerful shout
> Sent up for victory. I cannot tell
> What rare effect the mingled sound may yield
> Of huntsmen, hounds, and horns to firmer hearts
> Which never feel a pain for flying puss ;
> To me it gives a pleasure far more sweet
> To hear the cry of infant jubilee
> Exulting thus. Here all is innocent,
> And free from pain. *

Milton's nephew, Edward Phillips, notices cricket in 1685. One of the songs—"Of a noble race was Shenkin"

---

* Rev. Dr. Hurdis' *Village Curate*, p. 50.

—in Tom D'Urfey's *Pills to Purge Melancholy*, commences thus—

> Her was the prettiest fellow
> At football or at cricket.

Pope and Swift both allude to the game. It was played at Eton in Horace Walpole's younger days. The *British Champion* of 8th September, 1743, published an article on "Publick Cricket Matches," from which it appears that "noblemen, gentlemen, and clergymen" were then, as now, in the habit of joining with their social inferiors in playing the game; that notices of the matches were given by advertisement in the newspapers, and that large numbers of people flocked to behold them. The game afforded an anonymous poet in the *Gentleman's Magazine* for October, 1756, occasion "to point a moral":

THE GAME OF CRICKET.

An Exercise at Merchant Taylors' School.

> Peace and her arts we sing—her genial power
> Can give the breast to pant, the thought to tower,
> Tho' guiltless, not inglorious souls inspires,
> And boasts less savage, not less noble fires.
> Such is her sway, when Cricket calls her train,
> The sons of labour, to the accustom'd plain,
> With all the hero's passion and desire,
> They swell, they glow, they envy, and admire;
> Despair and resolution reign by turns;
> Suspense torments, and emulation burns.
> See! in due rank dispos'd, intent they stand,
> In act to start—the eye, the foot, the hand,
> Still active, eager, seem conjoin'd in one;
> Tho' fixt, all moving, and while present gone.
> In ancient combat, from the *Parthian* steed,
> Not more unerring flew the barbed reed
> Than rolls the ball, with varied vigour played,
> Now levell'd, whizzing o'er the springing blade,
> Now toss'd to rise more fatal from the ground,

Exact and faithful to th' appointed bound,
Yet vain its speed, yet vain its certain aim ;
The wary batsman watches o'er the game ;
Before his stroke the leathern circle flies,
Now wheels oblique, now mounting threats the skies.
Nor yet less vain the wary batsman's blow,
If intercepted by the encircling foe,
Too soon the nimble arm retorts the ball,
Or ready fingers catch it in its fall :
Thus various art with varied fortune strives,
And with each changing chance the sport revives.
Emblem of many-colour'd life—the State
By Cricket-rules discriminates the great :
The outward side, who place and profit want,
Watch to surprise, and labour to supplant :
While those who taste the sweets of present winnings
Labour as heartily to keep their *innings*.
On either side the whole great game is play'd,
Untried no shift is left, unsought no aid :
Skill vies with skill, and pow'r contends with pow'r,
And *squint-eyed prejudice* computes *the score*.
In private life, like *single-handed players*,
We get less *notches*, but we meet less cares.
Full many a lusty effort, which at court
Would fix the doubtful issue of the sport,
Wide of its mark, or impotent to rise,
Ruins the rash, or disappoints the wise.
Yet all in public and in private strive
To keep the ball of action still alive,
And just to all, when each his ground has run,
Death *tips the wicket*, and the game is done.

In 1774, cricket underwent some modifications, when a number of noblemen and gentlemen formed themselves into a Committee, of which the Duke of Dorset was the chairman, and drew up a code of laws for the regulation of the game, which only existed before in a loose and desultory form. From this cause, the year 1874 has been styled by some as the centenary of cricket."*

* *Notes and Queries :* 5th Series, Vol. II., p. 121.

The main point with which we have to deal is the precise period when cricket was introduced into Scotland.

Several towns claim the precedency.   It is stated that the game was played on Glasgow Green in 1817 and 1818; and that a club was instituted at Greenock in 1823. The Grange Club of Edinburgh dates from 1832.   Perth, however, can put in a prior claim.

The Perth Cricket Club was formed in 1827 ; but cricket had been played on the North Inch fifteen years earlier.   In 1812, the cavalry stationed in the Perth Barracks were in the habit of playing cricket on the Inch ; and at that time the boys of a public school formed themselves into a club, and pursued the game on the same ground.

It would thus appear that the " Fair City " has a good claim to be called the cradle of Scottish cricket, or, as the *Cricketer's Annual* (No. 2, p. 28) phrases it, "the birthplace of cricket in Scotland." *

---

* Sievwright's *Historical Sketch of the Perth Cricket Club.*

THE END.